I0210060

EVILS OF POVERTY

Revised Edition

MICHAEL M. CHARWAY

Evils of Poverty

Revised Edition

Copyright © 2021 by Michael Charway

All rights reserved. No part of this book may be reproduced or transmitted in any form or by any means, electronic or mechanical, including photocopying, recording, or by any information storage and retrieval system, without written permission of the publisher.

ISBN

Paperback: 978-1-77419-068-5

Ebook: 978-1-77419-075-3

MAPLE LEAF PUBLISHING INC.

3rd Floor 4915 54 St Red Deer,

Alberta T4N 2G7 Canada

General Inquiries & Customer Service

Phone: 1-(403)-356-0255

Toll Free: 1-(888)-498-9380

Email: info@mapleleafpublishinginc.com

Dedication

To All those who desires changes

for the better

Contents

FOREWORD

"Poverty is not an accident. Like slavery and apartheid, it is manmade and can be removed by the action" (Nelson Mandela)

"The earth has enough for our needs; not enough for our greed." (Quote)

"You can't feed the poor, but can fund wars" (Quote)

This book is about poverty and it's attending woes. The book in simple language reveals some of the causes of poverty and why it still persists. It tells us how tragically, most people have become so used and addicted to poverty so much that it has been "accepted" as a way of life. While many books has been written about poverty, it could easily be noticed that the authors of such books somehow always falls short of letting people know their own individual responsibilities concerning what they can do to get out of poverty.

With the exception of some who are born into wealth left by their parents or relations, most people have suffered poverty in one form or the other; the severity differs from one person to another. This book throws light on wrong teachings and beliefs which has resulted in people being misled about the real issues concerning poverty. Most importantly, the book offers us an insight into simple truths and things one can do to overcome poverty. If people have the right information, changes their mindset and act on the information, there is the posiibility their lives can be changed for the better. The writer encourages the reader not just to hate poverty, but to go all out and fight it. This edition has been revised from the original version.

THE POVERTY SCOURGE

"There is a powerful driving force inside every human being that once unleashed, can make any vision, dream or desire a reality." (Anthony Robbins

"The size of your success is measured by the strength of your desire; the size of your dream; and how you handle disappointments along the way." (Robert Kiyosaki)

Poverty is a dreaded disease all abhor. Strangely, it is tolerated and "accepted" by most people as part and parcel of society; no thanks to some people who teach that there is nothing anybody can do about it. Infact, some teach that it is the will and plan of God that some should be poor and mendicant, and trying to better one's life is against the will of God. It is this mentality that has made the ignorant to resign themselves to poverty and it's attendant suffering.

One only have to look around the enviroment to see the devastating effects of poverty. When we talk of poverty, we are not talking of somebody who is short of money and so cannot afford something at a particular time, but will come some other time to pick the item. We are not talking of somebody who can afford the basic needs of life like good meals, descent house or clothing and things like that, but maybe is not a landlord or a car owner. This is not poverty.

We are not talking of people who skips vaccation once a while. We are talking of a situation where somebody has been reduced to a state where one is only existing and not living. It is a state where somebody is litterally picking leftover food from dustbins and refuse heaps. It is a state where like the prodigal son, one desires the food given to animals so he will not die of hunger.(Lk.15:16) This is the stage where a human being has lost all sense of dignity and living without a shred of hope for anything good.

PICTURES WORTH A THOUSAND WORDS

"What a devil art thou, Poverty! How many desires, how many aspirations after goodness and truth, how many noble thoughts, loving wishes towards our fellows, beautiful imaginings thou hast crushed under thy heel, without remorse or pause" (Whitman)

"The world's hunger is getting ridiculous. There is more fruit in a rich man's shampoo than in a poor man's plate" (Habibies.com)

Browsing the internet to look for emblems or pictures I can tap ideas from for this book, I saw more than I have imagined. There are pictures so horrifying that your flesh will creep and your conscience seered with guilt; guilt that in this world where some have so much to eat and thrash, others will live in such deplorable conditions. The pictures are there in their hundreds, if not thousands, everyone of them depicting poverty in it's worst form and shape.

There are pictures of emaciated children looking like skeletons; with flies hovering all over their bodies. There are children with threadbare dresses that exposes more of their bodies than covers it. You will see pictures of bony children lying between the border line of life and death while vultures uncannily crouch some few feet away from them, waiting till they see no motion from those children; a sign for the vultures to move in. There are also pictures of ragged hungry children with a distant look in their tear soaked eyes.

There are pictures of whole families scavenging side by side with vultures, pigs and dogs at refuse sites for food and whatever they can find. There are pictures of men, women and suckling babies sleeping outside under trees, in large open drains, on the side walk of streets and other places; all exposed to the elements. You will see mothers whose breast has no milk to give to a suckling baby whose life, like the mother's, is hanging by a thread. You will see so many pictures of malnourished children looking very much like skeletal aparitions from a horror movie.

There are pictures of men trying to scare stray dogs away from a rotten meat at a trash site so they, the men can have the meat. You will not fail to notice pictures of poor folks living in "houses" which some rich folks will not ever allow their dogs to sleep in. These are houses made hazardly of mud and sticks with cardboard and leaves serving as roofs. The "roofs" of these structures are just some few inches above the heads of their occupants. Of course there is no electricity, running water or places of convenience in these houses.

There are vivid images of hungry folks who has fallen down where they stood a moment ago begging for alms or food; their begging bowls lying beside them. Others like them simply stood by, helpless to offer any help because they themselves are equally poor. Yes, there are pictures of folks who has made nearby refuse dumps their "source of supply." Day in and day out, they are there with dirty sacks looking for left over food to pick; these are real human beings reduced to these state.

There are pictures of dead folks lying on the ground while those alive could not even bury them, simply because they don't have the strength to dig graves; their own bodies reduced to skeletons for lack of food and nourishment. You will see pictures of emaciated human beings, deliberately placing themselves across railway lines so they could be run over by trains and so end it all. There are images of children about ten years old feeding a still much younger sibling with left over food picked from a trash bin.

You will see pictures of enviroments that looks like a bombed out village made of rags, mud and sticks with filthy stinky waters running amok all over the place. Strangely, just a mile or so away, you can easily see high rise apartments and luxury homes belonging to the rich juxtaposed against the filthineness of the poor homes; and you will see luxury cars of all makes and shapes driving past this poverty striken enviroments, the occupants of these cars looking straight ahead as if the villages do not exist.

There are images of men, women and children with thought provoking cardboard signs that read: Please I need a little love, I am starving, I am jobless, Can somebody show a little love?, My children are hungry, I need some shelter, Does anybody cares? I need those crumbs, Somebody should do something, Who will love me? Nowhere to go, I can work for a plate of food, No shelter and jobless, Alone and hungry, Homeless and scared, and so on.

The pictures seems endless, each one leaving an indelible mark on the conscience; if the conscience cares enough to be stirred into doing something to help these poor folks. But the question is, does society really cares? And if society cares, why is it that fellow human beings will go through such degrading situations of life while others have so much to eat and thrash what remains.

A QUESTION THAT NEEDS ANSWERS

"Make your life a masterpiece, imagine no limitation on what you can be, have or do" (Brian Tracy)

"All our dreams can come true if we have the courage to pursue them." (Walt Disney)

"Your problem isn't the problem. Your reaction is the problem" (Everyday Power)

What is poverty? This is a question which many people spread across all continents can easily answer without refering to any dictionary. It's effects can only be described by those unfortunate enough to feel it's deadly pangs. To start with, poverty simply defined, means a state of deprivation, not able to meet one's need and wants. It is a situation where an individual or family cannot fend for themselves and lack the basic necessities of life to live normal lives. It is a state where somebody always have to beg before he can eat. The definition could go on and on. So why do people easily resign themselves to such humiliating situation when they can do something about it?

Poverty certainly has been with humanity for a long time. Unfortunately, one reason why it has taken a foothold in our daily lives is because some deluded people keep telling whoever wants to listen, that poverty is a blessing and that being poor is a sign of humility. Over the ages, philosophers have synonimised poverty with being simple and good. Poets have expended pages upon pages to extoll the "virtues" of poverty.

Even some ministers of the gospel, misinterpreting scriptures, posit that man is spiritually high when he is poor; that the poorer a man is, the closer he is to God. This is a lie.

The question one needs to ask is: How can poverty and the attendant suffering it brings make people more godly? How can a man who cannot feed his family because of poverty be better off spiritually? How can a man who has been ejected from his apartment because of defaulting in rent and is now sleeping under a tree, exposed to the elements and cursing his misfortunes be spiritually higher than those living well?

How on earth can a mother of a hungry and malnourished child who is slowly dying before her very eyes, and could do nothing about it because of poverty, be spiritually closer to God? How can a situation which has robbed a man of self dignity and respect still make that person spiritually high? If the above questions are honestly answered, one will agree that poverty is evil and has nothing to do with spirituality.

POVERTY DEGRADES

"Whenever you see a successful person, you only see the public glories, never the private sacrifices to reach them" (Vaibhav Shah)

"A lamp doesn't speak, it introduces itself through it's light. Achievers never expose themselves; but their achievements expose them."
(Good Morning Quotes)

The poor is not repulsed by things that others abhor because he seems to be dead to all around him. He lives his daily life as somebody without hope. He doesn't care whether it is night or day; after all he has nothing at stake. He is pushed about by the whims and caprices of others because of his condition. Most often than not, he cannot react to insult or any assault on his person because the will to react is not there. He is never short of worries because it does appear that is the only avenue he has to let loose his pent up emotions

When a person is poor, he is always afraid of mingling with people. He is always in a constant state of inferiority complex, so he has a strong aversion for crowds. Crowds seems to add to his problems and woes. Anytime there is a meeting where people converge to share ideas and profer solutions to problems, the poor feels he has nothing to offer so he desires to stay back. Even if he attends such meetings, he feels intimidated and will not as much as open his mouth to say anything. If nobody asks him any question or talks to him, he immediately concludes people are ignoring him because of his pitiable condition. If anybody disagrees with him, the conclusion is just the same, it is because of his poor condition.

A poor man is always pushed about. He is serville. He does the most difficult job for the smallest pay and he cannot react because he is like a victim who has no rights. Because of the victim mentality he is living with, he thinks people who pays him for job done do not owe him any obligation, and that they are after all just doing him a favor which he should be grateful for. He even had to plead with people to pay him the right amount for job done and when the full payment is not effected, he is afraid to complain for fear they might decline payment all together; and that might leave him worse off.

When a man is poor, he is not regarded and respected by society. The Book of Eccleciastics 9:14-16 better illustrates this.

"There was a little city, and few men within it; and there came a great king against it, and besieged it, and built great bulwarks against it.

Now there was found in it a poor wise man, and by his wisdom delivered the city; yet no man remembered that same poor man."

This poor man by his wisdom saved his city from destruction when it was attacked from outside by a powerful king. The city savoured the victory over the enemy but they refused to recognize the man whose wisdom gave them the victory. Why? Because he was poor. The poor is never appreciated by society. Even when their wisdom is exploited for the benefit of others, society finds it repulsive to accept the fact that such wisdom enmanated from a poor person.

The poor cannot afford the basic necessities of life; right from decent accomodation to decent meals. Ordinary basic necessities that others take for granted is a luxury to the poor man. If he manages to cook, he may have to warm the soup every morning and evening for the number of days that the soup will last, because he has no refrigerator. He lives like a carion who has to survive off things that others have used and discarded; things that are meant for the refuse dump. He struggles literally for everything which under normal circumstance should be easily had. If he has children, they grow up without the benefit of education, thus putting their future also in the balance.

"The rich has many friends but the poor is hated of his own brethren." (Pro. 14:20)

Nobody wants to identify with the poor because he has nothing to offer. Whilst it is true that some people feel sorry and sympathetic, nobody actually wants to carry the poor along because they are considered as unwanted liabilities. After all, they can't make financial contributions if called upon to do so. Friends pretend they are not in when the poor calls because it is always assumed the poor is coming to beg for something. Neighbours act like strangers when the poor aproaches because they want to stay seperated from him. His presence or absence does not impact on his neighbors in anyway. As far as they are concerned, he is of no consequence to them.

"The brethren of the poor hate him. Friends go away from him; he pursues them with words yet they abandon him." (Pro. 19:7)

Imagine a situation where your own brethren hate you because of your poverty; where people who are your biological brethren ran away from you because they consider you a parasite. Can you imagine a scenerio where you pursue your friends with words, begging for their help and they abandon you, leaving you in abject helplessness. That is the lot of the poor.

Poverty imposes false humility. Most people equate poverty with humility. This is self delusion. Some people think just because they are poor makes them humble and heaven bound. They fail to realize that a poor man who does not know God is in the same miserable boat with the rich man who doesn't know God. It is not one's financial position that determines

17

one's spirituality, but his relationship with God. It is common to hear poor people say: "I came from a humble home." It is a lie. What that person is actually saying is: "I come from a poor home; all members of my family are very poor." When a man is in such a situation, he needs counselling; real good counselling.

When there is a problem, the rich talks harshly and with authority. On the other hand, the poor begs and enthreats.

"The poor useth intreaties; but the rich answereth roughly." (Pro. 18:23)

Poverty turns people into cowards; so much so that the poor begs the rich for mercy even when it is clear the rich man is wrong. Whereas the rich make demands and often gets what he wants by the sheer force of his personality and wealth, the poor can only beg to be seen; and even when seen, is still denied attention. The personality of the poor seems to repel rather than attract.

A poor man moves apologetically. His poverty has placed upon him a situation of permanent phobia. When he moves about, his body sends the message of sorriness. He behaves and acts as if the very ground he walks upon will arrest him because he is not fit to walk upon it. If he finds himself in any gathering, he has to hide himself at the very back. He feels the creeps whenever anybody looks at him in his threadbare attire. He lives with a persecution complex because he wrongly assumes that everybody and everything is against him.

THE ANATOMY OF POVERTY

"Don't let the fear of losing be greater than the excitement of winning" (Robert Kyosaki)

"Every accomplishment starts with the decision to try" (Quote)

"Work hard in silence. Let success be your noise" (Quote)

"Excellence is never an accident. It is the result of high intention, sincere effort, intelligent direction, skilful execution and the vision to see the obstacles as opportunities" (Aristotle)

Human beings and animals can easily be dissected to see their anatomy. One doesn't need any dissection to see the anatomy of poverty. It's visual effects are so pronounced on the body of those unfortunate to fall within it's tentacles. It's scars are scary and devastating. It is a wrecking machine of fearsome dimentions. Poverty is a dream nobody wants to come true.

Poverty does not discriminate between man or woman, young or old. It has no geographical boundaries. When it takes a foothold in anybody or anywhere and nothing is done about it, it spreads like a plague. You may go to a place and all the people in that place have the appearance of war ravaged victims; sickly, ragged, tattered, hungry, disoriented and confused. To them, nothing really matters again.

Have you seen a scene at a refuse dump site, where human scavengers rises up early in the morning to wait for refuse trucks to dump their refuse, so they can rumage through to see if they can find something eatable or worth taking? It is too hard to believe but this is true. The average person thinks of the next vacation; the poor ravaged person thinks of where the next meal is coming from and where to lay his weary head.

Watch those undernourished children with their bodies wracked with pains of hunger. They stand on the doorsteps of cardboard "houses" surrounded by muddy waters and filth. Electricity, running water and places of convenience are things they have not seen before. In some places, parents prepare their children for school in the morning. Not so with these poor children. Whilst the average child heads to school to learn, these poor children head to the nearest refuse dump site to see if mother luck will smile on them so they can get something to pick home; maybe a left over loaf of bread in a plastic bag. Theirs is a different world all together.

No matter how the poor tries to hide and cover his shame, his very appearance exposes his handicaps. Poverty is never hidden from the human eye. The anatomy of poverty is shame, rags, deprivation, hunger, preventable diseases, lack, reclusiveness, imaginary enemies, vain wishes and dreams that fleets away with the passage of time.

TYPES OF POVERTY

"I have learned that success is to be measured not so much by the position that one has reached in life as by the obstacles which he has had to overcome while trying to succeed." (Booker T. Washington)

"Obstacles are those frightful things you see when you take your eyes off your goal" (Henry Ford)

Poverty may be divided into three parts. The Comparative, The Religious and The Genuine.

THE COMPARATIVE: In comparative poverty, all is not lost because the person, though poor, is not very poor when compared to others. He sees some silver lining in the clouds. He has the energy and the will to struggle. When he compares himself to others within the poverty bracket, he is convinced he is better off than others.

He fights his poverty with the hope that if he struggles and fights hard enough, he can contain the level of poverty; at least, while hoping for the best. He even uses himself as an example to counsel others who think they are poor to think twice and fight on. Comparative poverty always make a poor man to be comparing himself to others.

The more he sees others he believes are worst off than himself, the more his hope rises and the more he energizes himself to keep up the fight. Positively speaking, if he tries and does the right things, his lot might improve and he may leave the poverty bracket and be counted with the middle class and hopefully with time, the very rich. Comparative poverty is "tolerable" if the one concerned can work his way out of it.

RELIGIOUS POVERTY: This is a situation where somebody in the name of religion deprives himself of all basic necessities of life. He lives the life of a mendicant, begging here and there. He does not hide the fact that he believes by going tattered, dirty and unkept, he will attract the mercy of God that will take him to higher spiritual levels. Don't be mistaken; this is not the normal abstinence from food and water which we all know as fasting; when somebody stays away from food and other daily vocations to seek the face of the Lord and ask for certain favors

This is self imposed poverty. Even though those in this category has the opportunity to make a living, they chose to wear the badge of poverty so they can get "closer" to God. Ironically, people with this thinking does not stop for one moment to ask themselves: "What if those I beg from decides not to work; who will give me the things I ask for?"

GENUINE POVERTY: This is poverty proper. It is a situation where the person is in a real pitiable condition. He is a pathetic sight to see. Anybody looking at such a one sees the very epitome of poverty with all it's attendant pains and woes. In such a state, the person does not know what to do or who to turn to because as always, the poor has no friends. All those who knows him turn their backs and litterally hide from him. He is at the very crossroads of life; confused, beaten black and blue by all the combined forces of poverty.

All social conditions are against him. He looks up to society for help but the system fails to answer his call of distress. Society looks at him with scorn because society only identifies with the rich and affluent; people they can get something from and not those who wants to be helped. Society treats the poor like a piece of rag; a rag so tattered and useless it is not even good for cleaning the ground. He cannot attend any social function, be it family or public because he is not welcome. As a matter of fact, his presence will cause some to leave or react in such a way that will send the message home to him that he is not wanted.

At this stage, he has lost all human dignity and self respect. He does not mind being seen picking things from rubbish bins. He cares less about being seen going out in rags or semi nakedness even though he is not mad. He goes to market places and rumages through dust bins searching for rotten vegetables and left overs thrown away by traders. He sees people he knows who pretends they have not seen him. He stares at them in the face and they look strangely at him, quickens their steps and leaves him wandering and wondering. Once in a while when a good Samaritan throws him a bite, he picks it with a mixture of gratitude and self pity.

He is not really bothered about how he looks or how people look and think about him. His only concern in life is to get a morsel of bread into his mouth to asuage the pangs of hunger biting his very being. When there is no one to give him food for his stomach, he resorts to stealing; not money or household gadgets but maybe a loaf of bread which cannot even satisfy a little kid. When he is caught, he becomes the object of laughter and scorn. He takes in all this with quiteness; after all what can he do.

Like a ship without a rudder and compass, he floats all over the place not knowing what to do. Sometimes, in the eyes of his mind, he sees himself in beautiful places. Such "visions" make the thought of hunger to receed far away to the back of his mind. But sooner or later, he is jolted back to reality when the pangs of hunger strikes. His is a very sad and miserable life, full of pain and hopelessness. Most people wake up the next day knowing where they will go or what they will eat. The poor doesn't have such dreams. He continues like this until he finds "release" in the waiting arms of death.

PROFILE OF A POOR FAMILY

"If you are not willing to risk the usual, you will have to settle for the ordinary." (Jim Rohn)

"Nothing can stop the man with the right mental attitude from achieving his goal: nothing on earth can help the man with the wrong attitude." (Thomas Jefferson)

It is almost impossible for some folks who has a car, a big television and some modern household conveniences to be convinced that they are not poor as they claim. They refuse to believe that what they consider as poverty is a party compared to what other folks are facing. Even though there are thousands of pictures and documentaries to back up stories that people are dying of starvation, and living in cardboard houses and scavaging at refuse dumps, most people, in the comfort of their homes still do not believe others are suffering more than they do. The following is a profile of a home striken with poverty; real abject poverty.

Jimmy is almost eleven years old. He comes from a poor home; a very poor home. His parents live in a one room mud house. He has two other siblings; nine and five years old. There is a heap of old and torn clothing at one side of the wall passing off as a bed. This bed is covered up by a worned out cloth that serves as a partition. They have nails stuck in all parts of the wall where they hang their threadbare dresses. The whole contents of their "wardrobe" can be seen and counted within seconds. Two wobbling wooden homemade stools sits at one corner of the room.

When the sun shines, the room is eeriely illuminated by the sun rays surging through the many holes in the worn out corrugated roofing sheets. It is worse when it rains, because they will have to put some cooking pots or whatever is available to catch the rain water dropping through the many holes in the roof, otherwise the whole room will be flooded. When evening comes, the parents retire to the "bedroom" behind the partition while the children stretch themselves all over the floor on some old mats. They have to manage a pile of rags as pillows. Real pillows are a luxury they can't afford.

The children gather and eat from the same earthen plate as there are not many plates to go around. Soft drinks are out of the question. It comes only once in a while; maybe, just maybe, at the end of the year. The children have to be satisfied with what they get to eat because it makes no difference whether they are satisfied or not; there is no more food to dish out. Even though you can see from the look in their eyes that their stomachs are clamouring for more food, there is nothing the parents could do about it. They have to fill whatever space is left in their tummies with water; plenty of it.

There is no electricity, no fridge or any electronic gadget in the house. Left over food is kept in a small homemade cupboard and warmed over and over again till they finish eating it. It does not matter or make any difference if the food is sour. The rule is that, nothing should be thrown away. Sometimes the stew or soup has to be continuosly diluted with water so it can go the extra mile and last longer. The house stinks with an uncanny odour enmanating from leftover foods and the stuffiness of the small room.

Believe it or not; things are so bad that for the children, there is nothing like a casual wear or dresses for occasions. All they

26

have is the threadbare dresses they wear everyday. There are no backup dresses. Most children boasts of having many pairs of shoes; not Jimmy and his sibblings. They can't afford such luxury. What they spot on their feet could well be described as straps of old leather bound together to resemble a footwear with the heels gone half way through. Jimmy has no idea of what a public play ground looks like. His shabby appearance made him look pitiable and silly. Even in his young mind, he can easily comprehend that all is not well with his family.

The only friends Jimmy has are just like him; poor and unknown. They play games of football or rather, something that looks like a football. The "ball" is made of strips of rags rolled together until it forms a sizeable round object, which they put into an old socks and ties the mouth to prevent the rags from falling out. This ball becomes their treasured toy till it wears out with usage. Even as they play at their game, they do not fail to notice that passers by slows down a little to look at them with some amused smiles on their faces and walks off. They are also aware that some kids from well to do families scoff at them as they pass by.

Jimmy's family go to bed early. The reason is simple. They have no eletronic gadgets like television or video games to while away their time. For them, there is no past time; no vacation or holidays. From sun up to sun down, theirs is a struggle for survival. Sometimes the children fidgets with some broken toys they picked from refuse dumps. There is an old rickety bicycle tucked in one corner of the room. It has no tires. Most of the parts are missing. Jimmy often sits on the bare seat and pretends to be riding. It gives him some sort of joy, but that bicycle is like a rocking chair; it only keeps him busy going back and forth but takes him nowhere.

When ailment of any form strikes, it is simply a moment of confusion, distress and much anxiety, because the family simply resigns themselves to fate. The only thing they do is hurdle around the sick one and speak some words of comfort and encouragement. Money to buy ordinary off the shelf medication is certainly not there; and there is no friend or relation to turn to. Most often than not, they turn to local remedies which has been passed on from generation to generation; namely leaves, roots and barks of trees which seem to work.

This is a composite picture of poverty striken homes and families. A poverty so grave that it defies all human understanding. People who spend thousands of dollars grooming their pet dogs and cats simply will not believe some people are litterally eating from dust bins. These rich folks, while admitting that some may not be as rich as themselves, simply refuses to believe that there are people who go to bed not knowing where the next meal will come from.

One cannot really fault such thinking, because when you live in a big house with so many rooms to spare, when you spend thousands of dollars on your pet dogs and cats, when you go on expensive vacations every now and then, when you have enough to eat and throw away, when you have exotic cars lined up in your big mansion, when you spend hard cash on manicures and pedicures, it is hard to believe that there is a family of four cramped in one single room with no food to eat and scavenging at refuse dumps.

WHY SOME ARE POOR

"There are two types of people who will tell you that you cannot make a difference in this world; those who are afraid to try and those who are afraid you will succeed."(Ray Goforth)

"Your mind is a powerful thing. When you fill it with positive thoughts, your life will start to change."(Kushandwizdom)

While there are a thousand and one reasons why some are poor, some reasons stand out above others. Some are high-lighted here.

LAZINESS: The Book of Proverbs 26:14 has this to say.

"As the door turneth on it's hinges, so does the lazy man upon his bed."

 The lazy man is busy for nothing; just going to and fro. He swings like a rocking chair; and of course a rocking chair will only get you busy but it can take you nowhere. He is always in full motion but no clear direction. Full of activity but no real purpose. Full of conversation but not discussing positive issues. That is the lot of the lazy man. Laziness can manifest right in the house where the house decays because of idleness.

"By much slothfulness, the building decayeth; and through idleness of the hands the house droppeth through." (Eccle. 10:18)

The lazy man hideth his hands in his bosom and will not so much as bring it to his mouth again. (Pro.19:24, Pro. 26:15)

How can a man put his hands between his legs, refuses to work and still believe he will prosper. That is certainly a wishful thinking. Hands are working instruments. A man who cannot put his hands to use will go hungry and beg for food. Life does not give you what you want; life gives you what you worked for. For example, if you want education, you go to school; you don't just sit down and expect to be educated.

The bells toll for the sluggard to rise up early in the morning and work; but no, he keeps on sleeping. He opens his eyes once in a while to check the time and convinces himself there is more time; so he closes his eyes and goes back to sleep. Here is what the scriptures says about such a person.

"How long will thou sleep, oh sluggard? When will thou arise out of thy sleep? Yet a little sleep, a little slumber, a little folding of the hands to sleep. So shall thy poverty come as one that travailleth and thy want as an armed man." (Pro. 6:9-11, Pro.24:33-34)

Laziness will always cause a man to have deep sleep and idleness will always cause a man to suffer hunger.

"Slothfulness casteth into a deep sleep; and an idle soul shall suffer hunger." (Prov. 19:15)

The lazy man roasteth not that which he took in hunting; but the substance of a diligent man is precious. (Pro. 12:27)

What an irony. That a man has substance in his hand that could be of use to him if he puts it to good use; but because of laziness, he neglects and wastes such opportunities. It is like somebody who has an interview by 9 am for a job but still in bed by 10 am. Somebody gives him a capital to start a business but he puts the money somewhere and forgets it till the money looses value or get misused along the line.

The lazy man is always giving excuses why he cannot move on. Somehow, he seems to have ready made excuses for his lack of success.

"There is a lion without; I shall be slain in the street" (Pro. 22:13, Pro.26:13)

Everybody is out on the street working; he is the only person who sees lions everywhere. Everybody sees oppotunities outside; he is the only one who sees failures and problems which is beyond control. He will always give reasons why he cannot make it. He simply refuses to take initiatives that will improve his life.

The world of the sluggard is a world of wishful thinking. He keeps on desiring what he cannot get; hoping it will come somehow, but nothing comes. Of course you cannot reap where you have not sown, but this means nothing to the lazy man. He believes he can sit down doing nothing and simply wish things into his life. It is not possible. Wishes are not horses so the lazy ones cannot ride.

One result of laziness is that there is lack of achievement and self fulfilment.

"The sluggard will not plow by reason of the cold; and therefore shall beg in harvest and have nothing" (Pro. 20:4)

The farm of the lazy man is always negleted and overgrown with thorns and the fences broken down." (Pro. 24:30-31)

At a time when others are harvesting, the lazy man will have nothing to harvest because he has planted nothing, and therefore will be begging others and will have nothing.

In the Holy Scriptures, the apostles warns against laziness and did not hesitate a moment to lay a command concerning work.

"For even when we were with you, this we commanded you, If any would not work, neither should he eat." (2 Thess. 3:10)

Funnily enough, the lazy man always thinks he is wiser than everybody. He deceives himself that he knows better than everybody put together. Proverbs 26:16 renders it properly.

"The sluggard is wiser in his own conceit than seven men that can render a reason."

It does not matter the advice you give him; you are wasting your time. He deceives himself that he knows more than anybody and is not ready to listen to any advice.

2. **REFUSING TO GET OUT**: Some people remain poor because they refuse to get out of the poverty mentality in their family. You have a whole family line where there is no one person of substance. If one is confronted with a problem as often is the case, there is not one single person in the family you can go to for help.

The whole family can only be identified by the description of poverty. One could have thought that the most logical thing to do is to seek to get out and find ways to better one's lot and the family, but no, what you hear is: "I will not move out. I will remain where I am. I will manage. Ours is a humble family." So the poverty line continues.

3. **WRONG NOTIONS** that it is the will of God for them to be poor; that some are born to be rich and some poor. They believe if God wants them to be rich, He would have done so. After all He sees their plight and He has the power to reverse their adverse positions. They erroneously believe that trying to be rich is going against the will of God. Because they always hear wrong teachings to support their beliefs, they resign themselves to their fate.

4. WASTING TIME WITH VAIN PERSONS. *"For we hear that there are some which walk among you disorderly, working not at all, but are busybodies.*

Now them that are such we command and exhort by our Lord Jesus Christ, that with quiteness they work, and eat their own bread." (2 Thess. 3:11–12)

"You may never know what results come of your actions, but if you do nothing, there will be no results" (Quote)

Instead of spending their time profitably, some people spend their time revelling with vain people. They will neglect their own vocations to be following friends on party sprees; from club to club and from one social function to another. They call it enjoyment. While others toil night and day to put the means of their livelihood on better footing, the prodigals choose to waste whatever is in their hands on riotous living. The years rolls by and suddenly it dawns on them that poverty has come to stay. That is when they realise that:

"He that tilleth his land shall have plenty of bread; but he that followeth after vain persons shall have poverty enough" (Pro. 28:19)

5. THE **WRONG SIDE OF FAITH**: Some are poor because of erroneous beliefs concerning faith. They believe that by faith they will have everything they want, whether they work or not. That is not right. That is abuse of faith. A careful look at the Holy Scriptures shows that great men of faith were all hard workers who worked hard on their farms, planting and raising livestocks. Is it Abraham, Job and others? They were all hard workers.

They did not sit down with arms folded waiting for faith to put food on their tables. Even when manna and quails fell from heaven for the Israelites, the people have to go out and collect them in the fields. They did not sit down in their tents

33

exercising their faith for the manna to come into their homes. They have to go out and gather it. That is work. (Exodus 16:1-18)

God will certainly give us the ingredients to bake the bread but we have to bake the bread ourselves. Faith will not bake the bread or carry bucket to fetch water for anybody. When one refuses to put his hands to use and be useful to himself and society, that is not faith; it is laziness and abuse of self. Poverty is the result.

6. **IMPULSE PURCHASES**: This is a case of people buying and buying without any thought of investment. When they have exhausted their own money, they go about borrowing more money to acquire more things. The problem here is that they have no time to evaluate purchases; if they really need what they are buying. Everything they see catches their fancy; they must buy it by all means. Their houses has become like an unkept overcrowded mini warehouses, with all manner of things scattered all over the place. Buying has become an obsession.

Gradually, their resources becomes dry, because wealth which is spent and not added to will soon finish. So gradually the money diminishes and all too soon all together gone. Very soon, the people they borrowed from start to pull them left and right for their money. What happens is that they begin to sell the things they have bought at give away prices in order to settle their debts. Before you know what is happening, they are in such a pitiable condition that people who has not known them before would not believe, if told, that such people has seen wealth before. At this stage, one can only draw the curtain of sympathy over such persons.

7. **OBSERVER MENTALITY** comes when a man continues to look at situations and circumstances around him and refuses to invest in anything because of the fear of the unknown. Maybe they have seen people who failed in business for one reason or the other; farmers who planted and lost their crops

because of drought, or people who got swindled by business partners and so on.

They cite this and other reasons why they cannot go into any business. What they fail to recognize is that by sitting down and doing nothing, they create room for poverty to creep in. In this case, the greatest hindrance to self improvement are themselves. They have allowed other people's failures to stagnate them instead of challenging them to aspire to succeed where others have failed.

Most people are poor because when their dreams doesn't fruit in time, they become frustrated and allow disappointment to creep in. When they don't see instant dividends from their invesments, they give up completely and allow their failures to give credence to other people's failure; that it is not possible to succeed. When proded on to try their hands on something, they are quick to point at others who has failed and use that as an excuse why they cannot do anything.

8: **STOLEN WATERS**: Some are poor because of their deceitful nature; cheating others and betraying confidences. People do business with them and they cheat their way out. They refuse to give to others what rightly belongs to them and pass it off as being smart. What does not occur to them is that:

"Bread of deceit is sweet to a man, but afterwards his mouth shall be filled with gravel." (Pro. 20:17)

"Wealth gotten by vanity shall be diminished: but he that gathereth by labour shall increase" (Prov. 13:11)

Any money you get through cheating has a curse on it. It looks alright at the moment, but sooner or later, a business empire that is based on falsehood, exploitation and deceit starts crumbling. Money is lost in strange circumstances as if spirited away. Sooner or later, the law equally catches up with the person and made to face the consequences of his actions. There are many examples of these. The stolen waters which was sweet before has now become bitter.

"Stolen waters are sweet, and bread eaten in secret is pleasant. But he knoweth not that the dead are there; and that her guests are in the depths of hell. (Pro. 9:17-18)

9.**SALE OF DREAMS**: So many people have ambitions, dreams and visions of what they want to do, but like Essau, they have no qualms selling their ideas to others for a mess of pottage. They spend sleepless days and nights on blue prints that will catapult them to better heights, but the enemy comes and in a subtle way snatches the idea away. At that material time, it doesn't really seem to matter, but sooner or later, like Essau, they suddenly realize the importance of what they have traded away almost for nothing. Regrets sets in but it is too late. (Gen. 25:31-34, Heb. 12: 16-17)

Stories abound about people who discussed their intentions and ideas about some ventures they wanted to embark on. The people they discussed with discouraged them and gave them reasons why they should not embark on such ventures. Of course they relaxed and too late, they found out that those who discouraged them from embarking on those venture has taken up the same ventures themselves and doing very well.

10. **NOT KNOWING WHAT TO DO**: Some people do not start at all. Not because they don't want to but because they don't know what to do. They lack the idea necessary for taking initiatives. They keep on living like this while the years roll by until time takes it's toil on them. Too late, they realize their years has been wasted just day dreaming.

11. **COPYING OTHERS**: Some has formed the habit of comparing themselves to others. They want to buy what others buy. They want to wear what they see on others. Precious funds that should

have been used to initiate projects or business, which would have yielded some good returns are used or rather misused to buy things that at best, would pass off as luxury. When the dust finally settles, one is heavily in debt, all because of trying to be seen as affluent.

It is the height of foolishness for anybody to try to copy others just to be seen as belonging to the high class. There is no need for that. To start with, you don't know how others make their money. If they earn more than you, it is logical they will outspend you anyday. If they make less expenses than you do, it is logical they will have more remaining in their pockets than you do. Maybe they have money coming from other sources which you don't know. There is no reason why you should copy their life style and drive yourself into unnecessary debts.

12. **MEDIOCRITY**: This is a state where somebody does not have the ability to do anything right. The person cannot just bring himself to maturity to know what to do. Even when you give them opportunites and the chance to do something that will improve their lives, they will always make a mess of such opportunities. Position is given to them and they easily prove their incompetence. There is no improvement in their life style. To make matters worse, They are not even prepared to learn and do the right thing. All this means that they are stagnant in life.

SELF INDUCED POVERTY

"It always seems impossible until it's done. (Nelson Mandela)

"Don't make excuses for why you can't get it done. Focus on all the reasons why you must make it happen" (Averstu. com)

"Every morning, you have two choices: Continue to sleep with your dreams or wake up and chase them." (Quote)

While it could be easily agreed that there is some form of poverty and disease in every country, the level of poverty and disease in some third world countries certainly defies human comprehension. People are litterally living under such deplorable conditions that will send cold chills through your body. Preventable diseases like malaria and others which has been eradicated in most countries are still ravaging and killing thousands in these countries.

It is very common to see malnurished children in threadbare dresses, barefooted and unkept, scavaging for food all over the place. There are houses where the children never know when it is their birthday. Some children are so impoverished that they stare in disbelief and awe whenever they come across affluent and well dressed children. Poverty related sicknesses and death in this countries are staggering, thus destroying whole future generations.

So who is to blame for the human tragedy in these countries? Of course those countries always blame the West for their woes.

They blame the West for using negative propaganda to paint them in bad colors. Whilst there is some elements of truth in such statements, it must be admitted by fair minded people that most of the economic woes in these countries are caused by bad and corrupt governments, lack of accountability, misused of natural resourses, lack of vision on the part of leaders, internal displacement of citizens due to rebel activities, military coups and bad leaders who refuse to yield power to others.

In these countries, you have thousands of internally displaced persons with no hope of ever returning to their homes. Wealth that has taken years to accumulate and invest is destroyed, and livestocks rustled by marauding parties who often call themselves freedom fighters. When things like this happens, the already bad economies of these impoverished nations cannot of course feed the extra mouths made homeless and hungry. The result is that the poverty circle is widened to unmanageable dimensions.

Every year, billions of dollars from western nations and Europe go to these countries in aid programmes. What happens to these monies? Suffice to say that the greater part of aid monies are not used for the intended purposes. Most often than not, it is spirited away by those in power; leaving the poor and the diseased in worst conditions than before. You go through the cities of these countries and you will be suprised at the lack of basic public amenities; even when foreign aid groups has donated money to put up these amenities.

Then comes the independence celebrations; the leaders of these countries who cannot provide the basic necessities for their citizens will spend millions to celebrate independence anniversaries. They will hold flamboyant parties and invite foreign dignitaries to come and watch military parades and other frivolities. All these in the midst of hunger and deprivation. When the celebrations ends, they set up presidential panels to find out how the millions was spent. In all this, the poor folks fare no better.

The sum total of all this is that, these governments, either by omission or commision, has and still contributing to the suffering of their citizens. Anybody from amongst the citizenery who complains about such things is labelled as unpatriotic and a stooge of the West. In such an enviroment, there is no middle class or whatever. If you are poor, you are very poor; and if you are rich, you are very rich.

A MUCH DEEPER PROBLEM

"Success is no accident. It is hard work, perseverance, learning, studying, sacrifice, and most of all, love of what you are doing."
(Pele)

"If you really want to do something, you will find a way. If you don't you will find an excuse." (Jim Rohn)

"Success is easy to achieve once you set your mind on specific goals." (Atticus Aristotle)

In looking at poverty, one will see that most people are a problem to themselves than the issue of poverty itself. It is common to see poor folks who feels sorry for themselves. They feel life has no meaning. Infact they hate themselves. They hate the world. They hate everything and most of all they hate the rich folks; they believe they are poor because the rich is rich at their expense. With this mindset, it is no wonder most folks continue to wallow in the abyss of poverty with no solution in sight.

When one is facing a problem, the most logical thing to do is the right thing; try your best to solve the problem and not to resign yourself to it and feeling sorry for yourself everyday. Some poor folks spend all their time letting everybody know how they are suffering; how they were born in poor homes, how their great great grandfather, who gave birth to their great grandfather, who gave birth to their father, who gave birth to them were all poor people. What they mean is that poverty is hereditory in their family and there is nothing they can do about it.

When one considers that poverty and begging destroys a man's self esteem and totally ruins his image, it is even peplexing and confusing to see people totally cocooned with self pity and thinking that the only way they can survive is to receive handouts from people. Perpetually depending on handouts to survive is certainly a wrong approach to solving the poverty issue. Strangely, you find out that this poor folks who finds begging acceptable will tell you that doing "menial" jobs to get by is below their dignity. So you see that they prefer begging to doing jobs they consider menial.

Some will go to oracles to consult with mediums to find out why they are poor. When this poor folks consult this mediums, they are not told to go and work hard. They are not given ideas that will change their status for the better. They are not told to exploit their God given potentials to improve their lives. No, rather, they are made to believe that others are responsible for their plight and society is not fair to them and so on. Now, in what way do the poor break the shackles of poverty with this kind of advice? Their condition of course gets worse.

Self pity destroys a person. Once it is allowed to take roots, it spreads over a person's entire life's structure and destroys him. Victory is not for the feeble minded. People do fall, but it is tragic to remain on the ground. All throughout history, there are records of millions of people who rose from the depth of despodency to higher heights of achievements. Testimonies abound of very poor folks, who through strength of character and great determination, worked their way out of their "hereditory poverty" to the pinnacle of self fulfilment and riches.

NEGATIVE FALLOUTS FROM POVERTY

"There are people who made things happen, There are people who watch things happen, and there are people who wonder what happened. To be successful, you need to be a person who make things happen." (Jim Lovell)

"Challenges are what makes life interesting and overcoming them is what makes life meaningful." (Joshua J. Marine)

There are many negative fallouts from poverty. This fallouts has become visible trademarks of the poor. Unless there is a reversal of fortunes, this traits continue throughout his life. Below are some of those negative fallouts.

1. POOR SELF IMAGE- Poverty makes one to live with inferiority complex. It makes one to look down on himself.

2. NOT BELONGING- It isolates one from people. Sometimes it is not even because people want to be far away from the person, but the poverty status makes one feel he doesn't belong.

3. RESTRICTS- Poverty restricts one from going far and decides which direction one can go. One cannot reach where others are and cannot talk the way the rich talks.

4. IT RUINS ONE'S REAL IDENTITY- It beclouds the real you. Poverty becomes a name tag by which you are identified. It makes people to focus on one's condition rather than your character and image.

5. RESENTMENT- Poverty imposes on people a two pronged resentment. You resent people because you think they are the cause of your poverty. They also resent you because they have a negative opinion of you. Either way, you remain the victim.

6. IT KILLS POTENTIALS-The poor die with dreams unfulfilled because they don't have the financial strength to carry their plans through. Those who could help stay their hands because of the personality involved.

7. IT MAKES ONE SERVILLE- It imposes false humility and makes one accept abuse without offering resistance. It enslaves you to the one dishing you handouts. It reduces your capabilities to react to issues even when it negatively affects you.

8. IT DIMINISHES YOUR VALUE-Poverty makes one think he is not worth anything. It belittles one.

9. FEAR OF THE UNKNOWN-Poverty creates the fear of something happening that the poor cannot confront. He is always asking himself questions like: What if I accidentally break somebody's property; how do I replace it? What if I hurt myself; how do I pay for medical treatment? What if somebody sues me to court; how do I defend myself? Poverty drains people of all self confidence and gives them a fear complex.

10. POVERTY STEALS RIGHTS-Poverty denies a person his rights. He recoils into his shell when denied what rightly belongs to him. He sees himself as a second class citizen. He simply refuses to fight back when his social and constitutional rights are being trampled upon.

11. EXPLOITATION- The poor man is always exploited by society. He does more work for less pay. Because he lacks what it takes to add a legal pep to whatever job he does for people, he ends up with less payments or benefits. The sad thing is that, he seems "comfortable" with whatever he is paid.

12. IMAGINARY ENEMIES-Poverty creates a mindset that makes the poor to constantly blame others for his adverse situation. He sees an adversary in everyone; even those whose goodwill he could tap for his betterment.

13. UNFETTED ANGER-Poverty breeds anger; a lot of anger. The anger is often pent up because there don't seem to be any single person to vent the anger upon. In such a situation, everybody is a target. The whole of society is to blame for his situation. Even when the poor stretches his hands to accept a handout from somebody, he is angry with that person.

14. DESTROYS THE DESIRE TO LIVE-When real poverty comes in, the deasire to live is thrown to the background. The person does not see the reason to live. To him there is no plan for to-morrow. To him tomorrow may never come. Though he sees a better tomorrow in his dreams, he knows very well that when the sun rises to usher in a new day, his condition will always remain the same.

15. IT IMPOSES A VICTIM MENTALITY-A victim is never his own person. He is pushed about by the whims and caprices of others. The poor feels the same. Somebody must always give him the order to do what ordinarily he could do without any prompting.

16. THE OBJECT OF "ATTENTION"-The poor always get dual attention. Some look at him with sympathy. They see him as an object that needs constant pity. While he has so many eyes on him which sympathizes with him, few if any, offers him any help. Others look at him with confusion; confusion because they cannot understand the dynamics that reduces somebody to total poverty. Needless to say, none of these attentions and scrutiny helps him. It makes him only feel uncomfortable

17. IMPOSES A FALSE SENSE OF HUMILITY- Poverty imposes a false sense of humility; of course this kind of humlity is not true. Humility is a virtue; it is a quality of the human character and attracts blessings and respect. On the other hand, poverty degrades and destroys one's image and personality. When you celebrate poverty as a sign of humility, you need some serious counseling.

POVERTY IS A HEALTH HAZARD

"Every gun that is made, every warship launched, every rocket fired signifies in the final sense, a theft from those who hunger and are not fed, those who are cold and not clothed. This world in arms is not spending money alone. It is spending the sweat of it's labourers, the genius of it's scientists, the hopes of it's children. This is not a way of life at all in any true sense. Under the clouds of war, it is humanity hanging on a cross of iron" (Dwight D. Eisenhower)

Poverty is a health hazard. When you see the enviroment poor folks are living in, you will understand why sickness is very prevalent. When the body lack proper food and nutrition, it becomes easily susceptible to disease and infections. One only have to look at the pain wracked bodies of those in poverty to see the reasons why poverty is a health hazard. The very filthy enviroment that poor people are living in makes the emergence of diseases inevitable. Everyday, according to some statistics, about twenty thousand children around the world die of poverty or poverty related diseases.

You go to whole villages and in this age of technology and so much advancement in every field of life, you will see people still drinking from muddy waters contaminated with all manner of things. Worse still, you will see folks standing and bathing in this same waters from which others are drinking. They also cook what little food they have with this same water; thus bringing about water borne diseases. The filthiness of the place equally brings to these folks air borne diseases. The health hazards inherent in all this is better imagined than seen.

In the poverty laced enviroments of these poor folks, minor ailments that could easily have been treated and cured with off the counter drugs could easily degenerate into more serious complications; all because poverty has made it impossible for them to afford this simple drugss. This is shameful and tragic.

BLAMING EVERYTHING ON THE WEATHER

"The test of our progress is not whether we add more to the abundance of those who have enough; it is whether we provide enough for those who have too little" (Franklin D. Roosevelt)

"I believe that if you show people the problems and you show them the solutions, they will be moved to act" (Bill Gates)

It is true that climatical conditions has contributed to draughts that negatively affected agricultural products and led to food shortages and so on. Sometimes torrential rains has flooded and destroyed whole farms. But it is also true that in this same countries where you have food shortages as a result of climatical conditions, the politicians, the affluent, their families and friends are not affected by this setbacks. It is only the poor folks who always suffer. When you see the affluence displayed by the rich, you begin to wonder whether they are living in the same country where the draught or famine is taking place.

For those who wants to always blame the weather for poverty, the question needs be asked: Is it the climate that is spending billions of dollars on military ware while millions starve to death? Is it the climate that makes politicians take natural resourses away from the poor folks, sell the products and use the money for their own ends, whilst the enviroment where the resources were taken from is a picture of abject poverty? Is it the climate that makes a politician take home a monthly emolument that can feed a poor average family for a whole year?

48

Is it the climate that breeds religious intolerance or rebel activities that sacks communities, destroys lives and properties, live stock, farm lands and leave people homeless and poor? Poverty, though sometimes compounded by natural disasters, is not an accident that just happens; it is caused most often than not, by man. Therefore man has the responsibily to own up and begin to do everything possible to ameliorate poverty.

DEALING WITH WRONG INTERPRETATIONS

"The only person you are destined to become is the person you decide to be." (Ralph Waldo Emerson)

"A successful man is the one who lays a firm foundation with the bricks others have thrown at him." (David Brinkley)

Some people teach the erroneous teaching that some has been destined to be poor and others to be rich. Unfortunately, some of this teachings comes from behind the pulpits in our churches. Some ministers quote some Bible verses to support the teachings that poverty is God ordained. But these scripture verses, if properly taken in context and explained, gives us a better understanding of what the Holy Scriptures is actually saying about poverty and the poor. Here are some few examples.

PROVERBS 22:2 "The rich and the poor meets together, the Lord is the maker of them all."

The above scripture does not mean God created one man to be poor and another rich. What it simply means is that God created all of us no matter our station in life. For example, a man has two sons. One chose the path of honour and became a successful lawyer whilst the other chose to mingle with thieves and became a criminal. The fact that they chose and became different things does not erase the fact that they are all children of one father. Their father did not make one good and successful and the other a misfit; their choices did. This verse, taken in proper context poses no problem at all.

1 TIMOTHY 6:10 - *"For the love of money is the root of evil; which while some coveted after, they have erred from the faith, and pierced themselves through with many sorrows."*

The Holy Scriptures has never said having money is evil but the love of it is. It is the insatiable love of money that is evil. When a man reaches a stage where he lusts after money and is prepared to do anything for money, that person has a problem. When a person is never satisfied unless he covets what other people owns, that is evil. One only have to look around and see the evil that is being perpetrated by unsatisfied seekers of money to understand what the Holy Bible is talking about. It counsels that children of God should be careful and abstain from this snare of insatiable love of money in order to stay in the faith.

MATHEW 26:11 - *"For ye have the poor always with you; but me ye have not always."*

It is very easy for people to fail to understand the true import of this statement. Jesus came for a mission and He knows that He will live the scene after the mission while the poor will still be around with us after He has gone. All throughout His ministry, He did not fail to let his followers know that he will leave them:

"Nevertheless I tell you the truth; It is expedient for you that I go away, the Comforter will not come unto you; but if I depart, I will send him to you." (John 16:7)

"I came forth from the Father, and am come into the world: again, I leave the world, and go to the Father. (John 16:28)

Jesus was merely letting the people know that after He has gone, they will still have the opportunity to take care of the poor who lives within their midst. Jesus was not insinuating that of necessity, people must be poor. If anything, His statement was a call to all to take care of the poor amongst us.

ECCL. 12:8 – *"Vanity upon vanities, saith the preacher; all is vanity."*

Material things are things we need in our everyday lives. Houses, cars, food, clothing, etc; these are basic necessities of life. For one to say that possessing these things is sinful, is a misinterpretation of scriptures. Sure, earthly things will pass away with the passage of time through wear and tear or loss. All that is expected of us in life is to live for God and not put our trust in material things; for putting one's trust in material things is vain because they will pass away. A person need to know that true joy does not necessarily lie in acquisition of material things.

King Solomon is an example of somebody who certainly was very rich in material things; money, chariots, women and all that one needed to enjoy life. His fame spread far and wide. People from all over the place came just to see his wealth and wisdom. (1 Kings 10) He enjoyed his life to a level until he found out that life is not all about riches and fame. He saw how vain we are without God. The thought that material things will pass away is supposed to make us to properly place these things in our lives and not to reject them all together as evil. (Book of Eccleciastics)

MATHEW 5:3 – *"Blessed are the poor in spirit for theirs is the kingdom of heaven."*

This has nothing to do with material poverty. The statement is about the poor in spirit. The person is desirous of spiritual growth. He has the appetite for the things of the spirit; his desire is for the fruit of the spirit. (Gal. 5:22-23). This person is saturated by the very essence of the Holy Spirit. It is all about spirituality. He is hungry for spiritual growth. He sees himself as somebody who has not gotten enough of spiritual things and so must be continually and spiritualy fed so he will grow. The Book of Galatians 5:16 is always his guide:

"Follow after the things of the spirit and ye shall not fulfil the lust of the flesh."

Jesus did not say that in order to be blessed, one has to be poor. Poverty is not and can never be a guarantee to make heaven. The rich man who knows and faithfully serves God, believes in the Lord Jesus and the indwelling power of the Holy Spirit shall be blessed; his blessings has nothing to do with poverty.

PROVERBS 23: 4b- *"Labor not to be rich."*

The Holy Bible is not saying people should not be working, otherwise this will contradict what the Bible says in 2nd Thessalonians 3:10, that if a man does not work, he should not eat. Now, there are people who live their lives as if riches are the only thing to live for. All their labor in this world, they believe, must only be for riches. That is not right. There is a need to balance things properly in life. Money is not everything.

PROVERBS 11:28 " *He that trusted in his riches shall fall, but the righteous shall flourish as a branch."*

The verse is not against riches but the idea of people trusting in their riches to save them or make them righteous. Riches are material things we acquire to meet our daily needs and that of society. They do not save. For anybody to put his trust in riches is a danger that must be avoided.

GETTING OUT OF POVERTY

"I can't change the direction of the wind, but I can adjust my sails to always reach my destination." (Jimmy Dean)

"There are no secrets to success. It is the result of preparation, hard work and learning from failure." (Colin Powel)

"You don't have to see the whole staircase, just take the first step." (Martin Luther King Jr)

RULE 1: ORGANIZE- To start with, organize your life properly. Dream big dreams and aim to bring them to fruition. Make a mission statement for your life. A mission statement is simply what you want to be, what you want to do and how you are going to achieve it. It is a blueprint for your present and future as far as self fulfilment is concerned. Without any mission statement, a man is just drifting with the tide with no clear destination in mind.

RULE 2: AVOID DREAM KILLERS- Here is what the brothers of Joseph said about him when they saw him coming to meet them:

"And when they saw him afar off, even before he came near unto them, they conspire against him to slay him.

And they said one to another, Behold, this dreamer cometh.

Come now therefore, and let us slay him, and cast him into some pit, and we will say, Some evil beast hath devoured him, and we shall see what will become of his dream." (Gen. 37:18-20)

Dream killers are those who tries, using various means, to kill your ambitions and truncate your potentials. Sometimes, out of envy and jealousy, this dream killers will want to destroy you completely. Most atimes, hiding their real intentions, they give you "good ideas" which is supposed to help you but which actually destroys your dreams. Others will come and tell you why you cannot succeed. They will give names of people who have tried and failed and are now poor; and for that reason you should stop what you are trying to do. Don't listen to such people. They are dream killers. Remember the dream may be delayed but it shall surely come to pass.

RULE 3: ALWAYS BE YOURSELF- Don't try to be another person. Be yourself no matter what. A duck is built for swimming; it can never run like a rabbit. The eagle has the power of flight; it can never make the same pace as a horse. The horse, despite it's power of speed, can never climb a tree. Never jump into any venture because you see others succeeding there. Before you go into any venture, sit down and properly analyze what is involved to see if you have what it takes to do it. Don't jump into any business without proper feasibility studies. Failure to plan properly may lead to financial consequences that might bring embarrassment.

RULE 4: BUDGETING- Budget for everything you want to do with money. Luke 14: 28-30 advices us to count the cost before embarking on any venture.

"For which of you, intending to build a tower, sitteth not down first, and counteth the cost, whether he has sufficient to finish it?

Lest haply, after he hath laid the foundation, and is not able to finish it, all that behold it begin to mock him,

Saying, this man began to build, and was not able to finish"

The idea is that, we should avoid a situation where the business get stuck somewhere because of lack of money and logistics overlooked. There are times one takes a loan from a financial institution to do business. It is important you know exactly what you want the money for and how much you want. Never borrow beyond what you can pay just because the money is there to borrow. Remember there is interest to pay.

RULES 5: CHANGE YOUR THINKING- It has been said, and it is true that man is the product of his own thoughts; he becomes what he thinks. Renew your mind against all those ideas that go against the will of God concerning your life.

"Casting down imaginations, and every high thing that exalteth itself against the knowledge of God, and bringing into captivity every thought to the obedience of Christ." (2 Cor. 10:5)

"And be not conformed to this world: but be ye transformed by the renewing of your mind, that ye may prove what is that good, and acceptable, and perfect, will of God." (Rom. 12:2)

Stronghold of negative ideas and things must be pulled down in your life. Negative strongholds are self made prisons that cages you and prevents you from achieving success and fulfilment in life. The idea that poverty runs in your family and there is nothing anyone can do about it should be jettisoned. Your mind must be refreshed with positive ideas and the knowledge that God wants you to do well in all things.

"Beloved, I wish above all things that thou mayest prosper and be in health even as thy soul prospereth." (3rd John vrs. 2)

Replace negative thinking with the overcomer's mindset. Tell yourself everyday that: *"I can do all things through Christ who strengthens me."* (Phil. 4: 13)

RULE 6: REMOVE FEAR OF FAILURE- Nobody wins a battle he believes cannot be won. If others have failed before, learn from their mistakes so you won't repeat their failings. Identify with those who have succeeded and learn from their ideas. Always believe in yourself that you are born to succeed. Fear is a subtle thief. It steals potentials and kills ambitions. Make fear an unwelcome visitor.

"For God hath not given us the spirit of fear; but of power, and of love, and of a sound mind." (2 Tim. 1:7)

RULE 7: IDENTIFY those who will be instrumental to your success. Remember God uses people to bless people. There are people whose ideas and expertise you need to tap. Don't see partners as competitors otherwise they will go away with their ideas. Take note of the fact that a tree does not make a forest. There is always interdependence.

RULE 8: USE MONEY WISELY- Don't borrow money to buy cosmetics, shoes, jewelery etc. Such will plunge you into financial mess when the time comes for repayment of such loans. Simply put, don't buy thing you can do without. Realize that some purchases are not worth the trouble. Evaluate the things you buy and prioritize your purchases; do you really need them? Don't buy things just because you can. Don't compete with others when it comes to buying; you don't know how they make their money.

RULE 9: MAINTAIN FINANCIAL INTERGRITY- If you are already in business, Don't use the money your business revolves around to make frivolous purchases. Remember the life of your business revolves around that money. Once you destroy that base, you have destroyed the life line of your business. Handle monetary issues properly, so you will not come to a situation where you have to use all that you have in settling debts. What happens when it is all gone? The business will certainly fold. Guard your financial intergrity with jealous passion.

RULE 10: FRIENDS AND RELATIONS MUST PAY- Don't turn your business into a free for all show. Your business can only grow and prosper when friends and relatives pay for services rendered. If you allow friends and relations to have a free reign into your personal business, they will not see the need to pay for what they buy.

Many people have had their businesses completely ruined and destroyed by friends and relatives. If you want to give out gifts to people close to you, it is in order and it is an entirely different matter. But let people pay for services rendered so you can guide and protect the financial intergrity and foundation of your business.

RULE 11: BE PATIENT WITH INVESTMENTS- It takes time for investments to mature; the same way it takes time for a seed to germinate, grow and bear fruits. There is time for planting, time to take care and nocture what you have planted, and then comes the time for harvest. All this takes time. Don't give up on your dreams and investments, for you shall be well rewarded in due season. Always remember that PATIENCE is a virtue that carries a lot of WAITING.

RULE 12: FACE CHALLENGES POSITIVELY-You must learn to face challenges. Most often than not, the pathway to victory is rough and tough. The beginning of a project may be difficult and may test your endurance to it's limits. You don't have to back out because of some teething problems which is normal.

Many of the inventions that we take for granted today wouldn't have seen the light of day if their inventors had given up because of opposition from skeptics and setbacks. History abounds with people who tried for many years in their quest to achieve something and kept on trying till they succeeded. Challenges should spur you on; it should never cut your dreams short.

RULE 13: KNOW YOUR POTENTIALS - There is a potential in everybody. You need to know your potentials and develop it. Talents or potentials may differ from person to person. Nonetheless, there is something in everybody that can take the person to higher heights if that person can discover himself. Don't sit down on your potentials belittling yourself.

Many of life's great achievements has come from people nobody believe has anything to offer. Don't be put down by anybody. Believe in the possibility of your dreams becoming a reality. Stir up the gifts in you. Employ the power of creative imagination so you can translate your dreams into reality. Close your mind to negative thoughts that you are nothing.

RULE 14: BE A HARD WORKER- *"He that tilleth his land shall have plenty of bread: but he that followeth after vain persons shall have poverty enough."* (Prov. 28:19)

If you must succeed in life, you must be a hard worker. Don't use working hours to play or go for vacations. All this must be put in their proper places. Success does not come on a platter of gold; and that means going the extra mile. Rule laziness completely out of your life.

"For even when we were with you, this we commanded you, that if any would not work, neither should he eat." (2 Thess. 3:10)

No amount of prayers will put food on your table if you refuse to work. Great men in the Bible like Job, Abraham and the others were all hard workers. Nobody becomes prosperous who sits down doing nothing and expecting miracles to happen.

"He becometh poor that dealeth with a slack hand; but the hand of the deligent maketh rich." (Pro. 10:4)

RULE 15: AVOID EXCUSES-As is often said, success doesn't need an excuse but failure has many excuses. Don't give any excuse why you cannot succeed. That is a trick of the mind.

Don't blame witches and wizards for your failure. Don't accuse your relatives as being the cause of your problems because they didn't help you with money. Such excuses will not help you.

Who helped the Wright brothers to come out with the aeroplane? Who helped Louis Pasteur to come up with pasteurization? Who helped all those great inventors and discoverers to come out with all the wonderful products we are all enjoying today? Against all odds they made it. There is no reason why you must fail. Tell yourself you must succeed no matter what. Convince yourself that if others have succeeded, you can also succeed.

RULE 16: TAKE NOTE OF WHAT PEOPLE NEED- Don't just walk about. Be very observant. All around us there are simple basic things people need to make life more comfortable. Seek ways to supply or make those things. For example, people need to buy food, wear new clothes and shoes, repair damages in their houses, service their electrical equipments, buy flowers for their porches, remove tree stumps from their yards, mow and trim their lawns; to mention just a few. You realize somebody must supply these needs. It could be you and that means you are making money.

You need to realize that most of the gadgets and other things we take for granted today are all answers to daily needs; which some folks saw and did their best to bridge that gap by seeking ways and means to provide those things. Do not despise small opportunities but rather, take advantage of them. Be fast in your thinking. Be creative and innovative. This is how inventions and discoveries are born. You could be the next Mr Ford of Ford motors fame or the Wright brothers and be celebrated. You could make a positive difference in the life of somebody and at the same time make money.

RULE 17: HAVE A KNOW HOW of the business you are doing. Study the market procedures, distribution etc. Place value on your product by proper advertising and good packaging.

Keep your eyes opened for opportunities so you can quickly take initiatives. Whilst you may not be an accountant by profession, it is important to have some knowledge of book keeping; otherwise you will be easily short changed by a clever book keeper who, with the stroke of the pen can easily alter the zeros from hundreds to thousands or maybe millions, leaving you the loser.

RULE 18 - MANAGE YOUR TIME PROPERLY - Time is one of the most valuable things on earth, yet it is often abused by most people. Everybody is given twenty four hours a day, twelve months in a year, three hundred and sixty-five days in a year and three hundred and sixty-six days in a leap year. What you do with your time is entirely your business. If you spend all your time in revellings and such like, realize that for every hour of your time that you let fleet by and not profitably used, it is gone and wasted.

If you decide to put off till tomorrow what you can do today, remember that time and tide waits for no one; and procrastination is a thief of time. Time is ever costant, whether you are on the move or not. Time will never slow down or move fast for your sake. For every hour that you waste, there are millions out there who are making it big because they make their time count.

Don't waste time, it is a precious commodity. Manage your time properly. Everyday when you wake up, make a mental or written note of the things you want to do that day and what time you need to do them. Prioritize them as the case might be. Don't just allow things to happen as far as time is concerned; be intentional in what you do with time.

RULE 19 - DON'T LET SETBACKS SET YOU BACK - Sometimes things don't happen the way you planned it. Sometimes you make mistakes or people you trusted for something did not live up to expectations. Sometimes there are negative turnout on investments. Maybe on the very verge of what you thought will be a big success, something falls out of place and a whole miriad of problems arises.

Don't let these setbacks set you back. It is no news that people fall, but the tragedy is when they refuse to get up; when they allow temporary problems to overwhelm them to a point where they completely give up and resign themselves to failure. The ability to get up during a race is a determinant factor whether you will finish the race or not. We have seen soccer marches where just some few minutes to the end of a game, a team comes from behind, equalizes and goes ahead to win the game.

RULE 20: BE A CHANNEL OF SOLUTIONS- The world is looking for people who can profer solutions to complex problems; and the world is ready to pay whoever has such solutions, no matter who he is or his geographical location. Joseph was a slave in Egypt, but what catapulted him to prominence and wealth? He brought about solutions when it was most needed.

Pharaoh had a worrisome dream which nobody could interprete. A former jail mate remembered that Joseph had interpreted his dream for him and everything Joseph said has come to pass. All this while, Joseph was in prison for a crime he didn't commit. The king had Joseph brought out of the prison to the palace. Joseph interpreted the king's dream and also told the king what should be done to avert the evils that the dream potrayed.

The king looked around and realized that the only person qualified to handle what was to be done to save Egypt was Joseph; so he put Joeph in charge and decreed that nobody should sell or buy except by the authourity of Joseph. He put a royal ring on Joseph's finger and gave him a position that litterally made Joseph the second most powerful person in the whole of Egypt. (Genesis 41:1-57)

Joseph was a problem solver. His being a slave did not stop him from becoming the second powerful man in Egypt. If you have the idea and solutions that is needed, even your enemies has no option but to seek and pay you for those ideas and solutions you give. Are there not consultants sitting in their offices and selling ideas to people who can pay for it?

Whenever there is a problem anywhere and people are complaining all over the place and not knowing what to do, seek to proffer solution to that problem. Bring out ideas that will help solve those problems and you will be suprise how you will be catapulted to a higher state of your social life; this is exactly what happened to Joseph. When you have what others need, they will pay fot it.

RULE 21: DON'T BE AFRAID TO TAKE DECISIONS- Life is all about decision making. If you are afraid of taking decisions because of the fear that things will not turn out fine, you will never get anywhere in life. Sometimes decisions we make don't turn out right, but we still have to make other decisions to correct the mistakes of the first one. Learn from your mistakes and don't let setbacks set you back.

RULE 22: SEEK WISDOM FROM GOD- Seek wisdom from God who give liberally to those who asked.

"If any of you lack wisdom, let him ask of God, that giveth to all men liberally, and upbraideth not; and it shall be given him."(James 1:5)

"....Wisdom is profitable to direct" (Eccl. 10:10)

"Wisdom is the principal thing; therefore get wisdom: and with all thy getting get understanding.

"Exalt her, and she shall promote thee: she shall bring thee to honour when thou dost embrace her." (Prov. 4:7-8)

There is no reason why you should be fumbling and making avoidable mistakes when the Holy Spirit is there to guide you.

You must have a grip of God's word. The thoughts that God has concerning you are not thoughts of evil but thoughts of peace; to bring you to an expected end. (Jer. 29:11) Close your mind to negative things and focus on the fact that God wants you to succeed in all things.

GIVE MEANING
TO YOUR LIFE

"When everything seems to be going against you, remember that the airplane takes off against the wind, not with it. (Henry Ford)

"Many of life's failures are people who did not realize how close they were to success when they gave up." (Thomas Edison)

Success is largely of holding on after others have let go." (Quote)

Stop feeling inferior. Seek to improve your life. No one can make you feel inferior unless you give them permission. Begin to see yourself functioning successfully in every area of your life. Stir yourself up and get away from the mediocrity stage. Seek to explore and do new things. If you want to break new grounds, then be ready to try on new things. If some methods are not working properly for you, then seek new methods so you can achieve the maximum results.

Whilst not despising small beginnings, seek to expand your horizon. Don't be satisfied with small things. Aim higher. For example, if you are a cashier in a retail store, don't remain there; rather, see that as a stepping stone to the next level. Go back to school if you have to after store hours. Seek information that will raise your standard of living.

If you are given a position which by all standards you don't qualify for or merit, then realize that necessity is placed upon you to improve yourself so that you can meet the demands of that position. The process of life is a graduation; that is, from one point to the other. That is why we start from kindergarten and climb up to college and other higher institutions. Your life must equally grow and improve.

Have a purpose in life. Don't just exist. Have a goal in life of where you are going. Make a mission statement to yourself concerning what you want to do, how you want to achieve your life's ambition. Everyday when you wake up, tell yourself: "In a week or a month or a year's time, this is where or what I want to be," and work towards actualizing those dreams. If you live a purposeless life without any mission statement, your life will just fleet away and before you know it, time has taken it's toil on your strength and potentials, leaving you with nothing but regrets.

Learn for a reason. Wearing the academic gowns is not so important as the reason why you are in the school. People don't go to school just for going sake, they go to school to seek information; to aquire knowledge they can apply to their lives so they can have a meaningful existence. Know why you are learning what you are learning. Put your soul into what you are learning, knowing fully well what benefit you are going to derive from the aquisition of the knowledge.

Take advantage of opportune moments that comes into your life. Don't let opportunities slip by without you recognizing and seizing them to make something good out of them. In the Holy Scriptures, Jacob encountered a man who engaged him in a fight. Jacob held unto him and refused to let go; The story reads:

"And Jacob was left alone; and there wrestled a man with him until the breaking of the day.

And he said, Let me go, for the day breaketh. And he said, I will not let go, except thou bless me.

And Jacob asked him, and said, Tell me, I pray thee, thy name, And he said, wherefore is it that thou dost ask after my name? And he blessed him there. " (Genesis 32:24,26,29)

Here we see that Jacob took advantage of a rare moment and refused to let go until he got what he wanted; the blessing. He recognized that this could be once in a life time moment and he took hold of it. This story also shows that he has spiritual sensitivity for him to recognize that this man he was wrestling with is carrying a blessing that he can tap from.

KNOW THOSE WHO WILL BE INSTRUMENTAL TO YOUR SUCCESS

"One of the greatest tragedies in life is the fact that many failures could have been turned into rich success if the people involved could have just made one more effort, tried one more time or just held on for just a few days or even minutes longer." (Quote)

"Don't make a cemetary of your life by burying your talents." (Quote)

In life's sphere, there are people who by virtue of their experience, knowledge, expertise and callings amongst other things, will be instrumental to your success if you recognize and get close to them. These people may come your way but if you fail to recognize what they can offer you, you may miss opportunities all together. Instead of being jealous or envious of these people, let their expertise and knowledge rob on you.

In the Holy Scriptures we read that, despite their differences, Laban, Jacob's uncle, did not want Jacob to leave him. He had this to say about Jacob.

"And he said unto him, I pray thee, if I have found favour in thine eyes, tarry: for I have learned by experience that the LORD hath blessed me for thy sake." **(Genesis 30:27)**

So you see that Laban recognized that God has blessed him because of Jacob. When you read the preceeding verses, you will easily find out that Jacob and Laban doesn't trust each other and all along, they have been scheming and outscheming each other; yet Laban has to admit that he was blessed because of Jacob. In Genesis 39 Joseph was brought into Egypt as a slave, but his master saw something unique about him.

"And his master saw that the LORD was with him, and that the LORD made all that he did to prosper in his hand.

And Joseph found grace in his sight, and he served him, and he made him overseer over his house, and all that he had he put into his hand.

And it came to pass from the time that he had made him overseer in his house, and over all that he had, that the LORD blessed the Egyptian's house for Joseph's sake; and the blessing of the LORD was upon all that he had in the house, and in the field." (Genesis 39:3-5)

Even when somebody was needed to oversee the distribution of food during the famine recorded in Genesis, Pharaoh turned to Joseph for help.

"And Pharaoh said unto Joseph, Forasmuch as God shewed thee all this, there is none so discreet and wise as thou art:

Thou shalt be over my house, and according unto thy word shall all my people be ruled: only in the throne will I be greater than thou.

And Pharaoh said unto Joseph, See, I have set thee over all the land in Egypt. (Gen. 41:39-41)

If you read the whole of Genesis 41, you will realize that it was Joseph's wisdom and expertise that kept Egypt intact throughout the famine years. Take note that Joseph was brought into Egypt as a slave, but his masters were wise enough to realize that his input is needed for the survival of the nation of Egypt. Pharaoh was the king but he did not allow his pride and position to deter him from seeking help from somebody who was his subject; a slave boy for that matter

You may have an idea about something but it may take inputs from others to bring that idea into fruition. For example, you may want to build a house, but you will need the input of others like brick layers, electricians, painters, plumbers and others if the house will stand. You may be carrying the seed of something great in you; that seed may be lying dormant until you know and accept those who will be instrumental to help turn that seed into a tree that will bear fruits.

STOP FIGHTING THE RICH

"Moreover the profit of the earth is for all: the king himself is served by the field." (Eccle. 5:9)

"However difficuilt life may seem, there is always something you can do and succeed at." (Steven Hawking)

"Your true success in life begins only when you make the commitment to become excellent in what you do." (Brian Tracy)

It has become common for most poor folks to attack the rich and blame all their poverty on the rich. This mentality is fueled by politicians, who in their desire to get votes by all means, pander to the poor and minorities by selling them the idea that rich folks are the reason why some are poor. So now we have a situation where the poor now nurse an intense hatred for people whose only offence is being rich. All over the place, you hear of wealth sharing; that is, money will be taken from the rich and given to the poor.

This is a false narrative because the rich will not become poor just so you will become rich. Things does not work like that. To start with, the rich folks are not your enemies. They worked hard for their money. Rather than fighting them, it will serve you better if you get close to them so you can learn from them. Take note that some of them have seen tough times before. Moreover, by hating the rich because of their wealth, you put yourself in a mental prison of the mind which tears you apart emotionally in a very negative way; which could even lead to violence against perceived enemies. This is not good for you.

While you see the rich as they are today, it does not occur to you that they were not always like this and that they are coming from somewhere. You may not know the pains, the tears, the struggles, the embarassments, the rejections and betrayals, trials and errors that they have gone through to be where they are today. If it is possible to sit infront of all these people for them to tell you their stories of where they are coming from, perhaps their stories will change your mindset and equally rattle you into some positive action to improve your life.

While it is true in life that some folks amass wealth through shady means and at the expence of others, it is not true that all rich folks are exploiters and so on. By alienating the rich from yourself, you are depriving yourself of ideas that would help you to make it to the top. Let the rich be an inspiration to you, especially those who rose from the ashes of despodency and defied all the odds to make it to the top.

THINGS YOU CAN LEARN FROM THOSE WHO ARE SUCCESSFUL

"Don't wait until everything is just right. It will never be perfect. There will always be challenges, obstacles and less than perfect conditions. So what. Get started now. With each step you take, you will grow stronger and stronger, more and more skilled, more and more self-confident and more and more successful." (Mark Victor Hansen)

"That some achieve great success is proof to all that others can achieve it as well" (Abraham Lincoln)

Success do not come to successful people by chance. They worked and applied certain life's principles to their lives. To start with, successful people are not afraid to take risk and invest their resources. They do not allow the fear of failure to stop them from investing in what they believe in. That others have failed in those same ventures does not stop them from taking their own initiatives. They realize that every life's endeavour comes with certain amount of risks; and they are prepared to take those risks.

Successful people don't allow disappointments to stall their forward movement. They may face some disappointments as other people, but they see such as opportunities to restrategize and reposition themselves for a better outcome. For them, disappointments are temporary road blocks or obstacles which has a short life span. They have the courage and the inbuilt capacity to face and overcome disappointments.

They don't waste their time on frivolities. They know the importance of time. They place value on time by making every minute of their time count. They have proper understanding of the times and seasons and are at the right place at the right time. They put things in proper order so everything will fit into their schedule; for them nothing is left to chance. Their everyday life is planned around time. They don't procrastinate; they don't put off till tomorrow what they know they have to do today. They are not swept away by the tides because they know the time of it's coming and preapares for it.

They are patient with their investments. They realize and know that every investment has an incubation period for it to come to fruition. While they sow for profit, they are not in a hurry to reap a harvest which is not yet ready, knowing fully well that harvesting a crop before it's time will actually waste the crops and minimize the expected profit. While other people sacrifice long term profits for temporary gains, successful people patiently work and wait for long term profits to come in.

They chose their friends carefully, knowing fully well that the people you associate with will either take you up or bring you down. They associate with people who has positive ideas and likeminded mindsets. You don't find them in the midst of riotous people and rabble rousers. They flock together with birds of the same feathers; people who are just like them. They spend their time with people whose ideas and counsel will take them to higher heights of success.

Successful people always seek knowledge, for they know that knowledge is power. They don't shy away from information and are always eager to learn new methods of doing things in a better way. They don't allow pride to stop them from listening to others who has something to offer. They are very attentive and good listeners, making mental and written notes of what they hear so they can go through them later.

They don't live careless lives. They are very intentional about everything in their daily vocations. They don't just sleep and wake up each day without a plan of what they have to do that day. For them, nothing happens by chance. They have a direction, purpose and dream for each day. They understand the enviroment and are always seeking for the things they can do that people need and are ready to pay for it.

THE BATTLE OF THE MIND

"When you change the quality of your thinking, you change the quality of your life, sometimes instantly. Just as positive words can make someone smile, or a well timed humourus quote can make someone laugh, our thoughts react to our world in real time"

The pessimist sees difficulty in every opportunity, the optimist see opportunity in every difficulty." (Quote)

"We don't realize the extend to which negative thoughts contributes to our mental anguish. The earlier you stop those thoughts from taking roots in your life, the easier it is to regroup and get back on track." (Quote)

"You can decide what you are going to think in any given situation. Your thoughts and feelings determine your actions and determine the results you get. It all starts with your thoughts; and I have found that inspirational words are a quick way to retune your thinking." (Quote)

No amount of sermon; no amount of talk or prodings will make you rich and get you out of poverty if your mindset is bogged down with negative ideas about riches. If you don't free your mind from negative beliefs, such beliefs will always reflect negatively on you. If you don't remove the cobwebs of negativism from your mind, there is no way you can make any headway in life. How do you explain a situation where some people believe that for them to enjoy in heaven, they must first suffer on earth. They believe while awaiting their rapture by the Lord Jesus, they must be miserable on earth, beg for food, sleep in ramshakled cardboard houses and deprived of all the good things that makes life comfortable.

They take pride in telling people how when they get to heaven, they will start enjoying all the good things they missed out here on earth. Despite all that the Holy Scriptures say about living the abundant life here on earth and in the world to come, most people are still lost out on this fact. This is the product of a warped mindset that needs changing. Here is what Jesus said to Peter in answer to a question:

And He said unto them, *Verily I say unto you, There is no man that hath left house, or parents or brethren, or sisters, or wife, or children, for the kingdom of God's sake,*

Who shall not receive manifold more in this present time; and in the world to come life everlasting" (Luke 18:29-30)

But he shall receive an hundredfold now in this time, houses, and brethren, and sisters, and mothers, and children, and lands, with persecutions; and in the world to come eternal life." (Mark 10:30)

So you see that God desires His children to live and enjoy the blessings which He has endowed the earth with.

"Moreover the profit of the earth is for all: the king himself is served by the field" (Eccl. 5:9)

"And also that every man should eat and drink, and enjoy the good of all his labour, it is the gift of God" (Eccl. 3:13)

Nobody is responsible for your thoughts. You are responsible for what you think. If you have made up your mind not to do anything positive and suceed in life, there is nothing anybody can do about it. Learning is of no use if your mindset remains unchanged from negative thoughts. You can get all the knowledge in the world; that knowledge is of no use if it is not applied. Not just any knowledge but right and profitable knowledge.

Everything is in the mind. All the inventions we see came from the mind; ideas all come from the mindset. If the mindset is not freed from the strongholds of fear of failure, wrong ideas, lack of understanding amongst other things, no amount of sermonizing will suffice. It is not because there is shortage of good ideas to make people better, but the problem is because people have closed their minds to such good ideas and allowed negative mindsets to take root in them.

Remember the story in the Holy Scriptures about the un-profitable servant. (Mat. 25:14-28) The master was travelling and gave him and other servants some amounts of money. Everyone of those who received the money traded with it and doubled his money. The only exception was the unprofitable servant. While others made investment with their money, he dug the ground and hid his own, thus making no profit. When the day of accountability came, he has nothing to show. Infact, he even accused the master of being a selfish person who wants to reap where he has not sown. Such is the mentality of failures. It's all in the mind.

Some people have made their minds that it doesn't matter what anybody says; they will forever remain poor and there is nothing anybody can do about it. Some even prefer begging to working. There are people with traits of talents and potentials, which if they put to good use, will put them on a solid finan-cial footing, but their negative mindset will not allow them. They have so much negative ideas in their mental make up that their reasoning power has been taken over by thoughts of defeat and despodency.

The mind is a battle ground for ideas; both good and evil; negative or positive. The reason why some are doing so well is because they have aligned themselves with the positive and good and decided to succeed. It took some people years of patience to actualize their dreams; yet some believe if they have failed once, they will always fail. They see failure everywhere. It is all in the mind.

The story is told of the guy who was sent to a village to market some shoes. He came back to his employers saying it is no use wasting time in that village because the people are backward and don't wear shoes. He claimed they have never seen shoes before and that the company has no future there. Well, another sales guy was sent to the same village and he came back with this: "We have a big market in that place. The people don't wear shoes; this is an opportunity to introduce shoes to them. The prospects are very good." You see, two people were sent to the same place; while one saw failure; the other saw opportunity to make it big. You see, it is all in the mindset.

Some have become so "spiritual" that they don't believe human beings physically has to put ideas on the ground to make things work. Such people live with the mentality of "What will be will be and there is nothing you can do about it." Their mind has been made up. They will not bulge. They forget that if they don't win the battle of the mind, they will perpetually loose the war against poverty. Whether they will succeed in life or not depends a lot on their mindset. They need to have a rethink and have a change of attitude.

BUNDLES OF CONTRADICTIONS

"Many a man is a bundle of contradictions, and trying to understand humanity is an excercise in futility" (Quote)

The general behaviour of people is quite strange when you consider the things we do, our reactions to issues of the day, and sometimes the total indifference of humanity concerning things that happens around us. This is why everywhere you look, especially in relationship to poverty and homelessness, mankind has become a bundle of contradictions; saying one thing and making sure everything he does is contrary to what he says. This is why man's response to the poverty scourge is anything but sincere.

We sponsor wars and conflicts but we complain of lack of funds when it comes to the issues of feeding the poor. We build amusement parks but will not spare a little space for the poor to build a thatch house to shelter himself from the rain. We donate millions of dollars to politicians but watch and do nothing when a poor folk is refused treatment at a hospital because he has no money to pay for medication. We spend thousands of dollars on our pet dogs and cats but will not lift a finger to spare a dollar for a homeless folk lying hungry on the street. We eat and thrash what remains, even while we watch emaciated children in threadbare attires go to bed unfed.

Every year, poor countries which cannot feed their poor somehow still manage to find and spend millions of dollars organiziing independence celebrations and match pasts, at which events the latest military wares are displayed. Not once do these countries parade agricultural machines that can help the farming sector and the poor. Humanity spend millions in beauty pagents but will not spend a quarter of these monies to promote health related programs for those who need it. In the west, politicians spend close to a billion dollars each on campaigns and still turn round and 'wonder' why the poor is getting poorer and the rich getting richer.

The rich and those in power will destroy farm lands and the homes of the poor to build luxury hotels, and still turn around to complain about poverty and homelessness. Politicians initiate policies that hurt and deprive people of their initiatives to do something for themselves, and still pretend they care for this people. This is why you have a lot of people dependent on welfare without any present or future financial security. This is so because politicians, in order to get the votes from this class of people, encourage them to stay on welfare and not find a job. This is a deliberate abuse of people.

All this means that, honesty is desired of everybody to deal with the poverty scourge. Governments should initiate real programs to help the poor out of poverty, and give them financial stability. The governments of the world should stop the wasteful spending of their nation's resources on frivolous independence celebrations, and channel those monies into farming, economic and housing programs. The politicians should stop the lip service and do what they promised the people they will do. The poor should not be robbed of their small backyard farms but rather encouraged and helped to expand. All that is needed now is for everyone concerned to put hands on deck so poverty and homelessness will be contained.

UTTERANCES AND IDEAS YOU SHOULD AVOID

"If you are working on something that you really care about, you don't have to be pushed. The vision pulls you." (Steve Jobs)

"The only limit to our realization of tomorrow will be our doubts of today." (Franklin D. Roosevelt)

"If you don't design your own life plan, chances are you'll fall into someone else's plan. And guess what they have planned for you. Not much." (Jim Rohn)

1. Poverty runs in our family. It is hereditory.

2. I am poor because I am under a curse. Nothing works for me.

3. Maybe it is the will of God that I should be poor.

4. Society is to blame.

5. I am being discriminated against because of my race.

6. Others have tried and failed, so why must I try?

7. I am not going to waste my money on such experiments. What if I fail.

8. I have tried before and failed. I am not going to try again.

9. Everybody and everything is against me.

10. He is lucky to have succeeded. I don't think I have the same luck.

11. I don't want to take any gamble with any business.

12. Some are born with silver spoons. I wasn't so lucky.

13. I am created like this. There is nothing I can do about it.

14. Poverty draws you closer to God.

15. All fingers are not equal. Some are born to be poor and some rich.

16. I am jinxed not to succeed.

17. Poverty is a sign of humility.

18. Poverty is natural otherwise it won't be there in the first place.

19. I am poor because the rich will not allow me to be rich.

20. I can't invest in this project because it will take some time before I start getting any profit.

21. No matter how hard you tried, you will not make it because some people don't want you to succeed.

22. Poverty has been with humanity for ages. Just tolerate it. There is nothing you can do about it.

23. I will be rich if and when I will be rich. There is no need to do anything.

24. Man is born to suffer.

25. Suffering makes people sober, humble and gives them a better understanding of life's issues.

26. What I have is not big enough to invest in any business venture.

27. I don't have what it takes to succeed.

28. It is all over. I have fallen too low and I don't think I can make a come back.

29. After so many failures and setbacks, I might as well call it quits.

30. Everybody agrees that poverty is part of life.

31. All the poor people in my life who tried to be rich were cut off at the prime of their lives.

32. I don't want to be rich and become the object of envy.

33. I am satisfied with begging. The little I get is alright for me.

34. Life is cruel and harsh for some of us. No matter how hard we tried, nothing works alright for us.

35. The rich must always take care of the poor.

36. All rich folks are exploiters.

37. The government must take from the rich and give to the poor.

38. I didn't get anybody to encourage me.

39. Friends and family members won't help me get to the top.

40. Why should I care? I am not the only poor person around. I am even better off than others.

41. The system is rigged against me.

42. The world is not my home so there is no need trying to have a good and comfortable life here on earth. I will be okay when I get to heaven.

THE BIBLICAL ANGLE

"I have been young, and now am old; yet I have not seen the righteous forsaken, nor his seed begging for bread." (Psalm 37:25)

Most people overlook the fact that it is the will of God for His children to live prosperous and fulfilled lives. Wealth is one of the many blessings God has established for His children.

"But thou shall remember the Lord thy God; for it is He that giveth thee power to get wealth, that He may establish His convenant which He sware unto thy fathers as it is this day." (Deut. 8:18)

Long before we were born, God in His infinite wisdom has already laid down the very foundation of our wealth. When we work hard and do the right things, God always give the increase.

God assures those who faithfully serve Him that *"They shall be blessed among all people."* (Deut. 7:14)

"Know the grace of our Lord Jesus Christ, that though He was rich, yet for your sakes He become poor, that ye through His poverty might be rich" (2 Cor. 8:9)

"But my God shall supply all your needs according to His riches in glory by Christ Jesus." (Phil. 4:19)

Knowing and remembering God as the architect of our wealth should make us thankful always. Apart from the blessing and riches that comes from hard work, there are some scriptural and material assignments that God wants us to perform so we will remain blest and blest indeed. The following chapters and pages will treat those obligations.

HELPING THE POOR INDEED

"No one is useless in this world who lightens the burdens of another." (Charles Dickens)

"Your greatest test is when you are able to bless someone else while you are going though your own storm." (Quote)

"We make a living by what we get. We make a life by what we give." (Winston S. Churchill)

"Those who are happiest are those who do the most for others." (Booker T. Washington)

As we study the evils of poverty and how to combat it, we must not overlook the fact that some are poor not necessarily because they are lazy or don't want to work. Some are poor and diseased as a result of natural occurences; earthquakes, floods, droughts which renders the land infertile, heavy storms that leaves destruction in it's wake, and other factors that humanity can do little or nothing about. Some are poor as a result of wars that has devastated the land and livelihood.

The after effects of such occurences could be devastating. Thousands are made homeless, businesses get destroyed and life time investments is wiped out in a matter of minutes. In a situation like this, the church should not only tell them to pick the pieces of their lives and rebuild them again; the church should really go out to help. Everything must be done in a practical way to help such people to get back on their feet.

It is not enough to shout from behind the pulpits. The church should practically take care of those who are really poor indeed, including the fatherless. Whilst the church will not condone laziness in people who refuses to work, necessity is laid upon the church to extend a hand of fellowship to those in need. In helping, the church is not there to give handouts on daily basis for ever. The idea is to help people get back on their feet so they can fend for themselves.

Isaiah 58:10 tells us to: "*Spend yourselves on behalf of the hungry and meet the needs of the oppressed; then your light will rise in the darkness and your night will become like the noon day.*"

The word "spend" is a familiar word to most people, especially those who spend big money on luxury items that only the very rich can afford. This time, God is calling us to spend on behalf of the hungry and the oppressed.

Leviticus 19:9-10 tells us that farm owners are commanded to leave some of their farm produce on the trees or leave them on the ground where they fell so that the poor or strangers passing by can have something to eat.

"*And when ye reap the harvest of your land, thou shalt not wholly reap the corners of thy field, neither shalt thou gather the gleanings of thy harvest.*

And thou shalt not glean thy vineyard, neither shalt thou gather every grape of thy vineyard; thou shalt leave them for the poor and stranger: I am the LORD your God."

True religion is to feed the hungry, take care of the fatherless, visit the widows and alleviate the suffering of those around you. Prayers alone will not put food into people's mouth. The Holy Scriptures clearly states that if you pray for a hungry man but refuses to feed him, it profits him nothing. He will still be hungry.

"Pure religion and undefiled before God and the Father is this, To visit the fatherless and widows in their affliction, and to keep himself unspotted from the world." (James 1:27)

"What doth it profit, my brethren, though a man say he hath faith, and have not works? can faith save him?

If a brother or sister be naked, and destitute of daily food,

And one of you say unto them, Depart in peace, be ye warmed and filled; notwithstanding ye give them not those things which are needed to the body; what doth it profit?

Even so faith, if it hath not works, is dead, being alone" (James 2:14-17

He who stops his ears at the cry of the poor will also cry one day and will not be heard. It is easy for people to pretend not to hear when the needy cries. As has been noted earlier, there comes situations in one's life which is not one's fault. It is the duty of all to help such a one get back on his feet. This is a divine assignment given to all of us. When a needy neighbor calls for assistance, you should not put him off when it is in your power to help him.

"Whoso stoppeth his ears at the cry of the poor, he also shall cry himself, but shall not be heard" (Prov. 21:13)

"Say not unto thy neighbour, Go and come again, and tomorrow I will give; when thou hast it by thee" (Prov. 3:28)

In Mathew 25:41-46, Jesus warns of the dire consequences awaiting those who refuses to extend a hand of help to those in need.

"Then shall he say also unto them on the left hand, Depart from me, ye cursed, into everlasting fire, prepared for the devil and his angels:

For I was hungred, and ye gave me no meat: I was thirsty, and ye gave me no drink:

I was a stranger, and ye took me not in: naked, and ye clothed me not: sick, and in prison, and ye visited me not.

Then shall they also answer him saying, Lord, when saw we thee an hungred, or athirst, or a stranger, or naked, or sick, or in prison, and did not minister unto thee?

Then shall he answer them, saying, Verily I say unto you, Inasmuch as ye did it not to one of the least of these, ye did it not to me.

And these shall go away into everlasting punishment: but the righteous into life eternal"

ATTRACTING GOD'S GOODNESS

"The young lions do lack, and suffer hunger: but they that seek the LORD shall not want any good thing." (psalm 34:10)

"Blessed is the man that walketh not in the counsel of the ungodly, nor standeth in the way of sinners, nor sitteth in the seat of the sconful. But his delight is in the law of the LORD; and in His law doth he meditate day and night. And he shall be like a tree planted by the rivers of water, that bringeth forth his fruit in his season; his leaf also shall not wither; and whatsoever he doeth shall prosper."
(Psalm 1:1-3)

For us to attract God's goodness and enjoy the best things of life, we must learn to walk in the ways of the Lord. The whole of Psalm 1 gives us a good profile of the man God blesses. Such a man must be the man who will not stand in the way of sinners, nor sit in the seat of the scornful or walk in the counsel of the ungodly. If a man delights in the word of God and meditates upon it day and night to perform it, God will surely bless and prosper such a one as He has promised.

If a child respects and obeys the father, there is every reason to believe that the father will not withold anything good from such a child. In Joshua 1:8, God told Joshua how He will bless and prosper him if he meditates upon His word day and night and to seek to do all that is in it.

"This book of the law shall not depart out of thy mouth, but thou shalt meditate therein day and night, that thou mayest observe to do according to all that is written therein: for then thou shalt make thy way prosperous, and then thou shalt have good success."

Some may ask the question: "If we need to know and serve God before we prosper, why are there people who don't believe in God, commits all manner of evil and yet are rich and prosperous? They posit that riches and prosperity will come to whom it may come regardless of whether the person knows God or not. Those who hold this view only have to look at the end of some of this people. Many ended penniless as if they have not seen money before. Some have to be running all their lives from the law. Psalm 73 offers a wealth of information concerning the end of the evil rich. Theirs are riches that comes with sorrow; their feet is set in slippery places.

"Bread of deceit is sweet to a man; but afterwards his mouth shall be filled with gravel." (Proverbs 20:17)

Some may be living a life of deceit, falsehood and aquiring riches by evil machinations, but sooner or later things turns out badly for them, and suddenly their riches become gravel in their mouth. These are the sort of riches that is kept to the owners travail. In contrast, for the child of God,

"The blessings of the Lord maketh rich and He adds no sorrow to it."(Prov. 10:22)

People need to realize that it is not the will of God that any should perish but rather they repent and accept the Lord Jesus as their savior. He gives the evil doer a long rope to change. (2 Peter 3:9) It ought to be noted here that evil people prospering does not rule out the fact that if they refuse to repent of their evil ways, a time will come when they will have to face God whom they have rejected.

"The righteousness of the perfect shall direct his ways, but the wicked shall fall by his wickedness." (Pro. 11:5)

"Trust in the Lord with all thine heart; and lean not unto thy own understanding. In all thy ways acknowledge Him, and He shall direct thy paths." (Pro. 3:5-6)

There is nothing wrong in having ambitions and thinking big, but it is the height of ignorance and pride to think one can go without God. One needs God's grace to go on. When you trust your plans into God's hands, He sure through the Holy Spirit will give you the right ideas and directions you need to go about your business. He will get you connected to the right people who will be instrumental to your success. In addition, He will cause His favor to rest upon you.

GIVING YOUR WAY TO VICTORY

"There is he who scattereth, and yet increaseth; and there is he that witholdeth more than is meet, but it turneth to poverty. The liberal soul shall be made fat, and he that watereth shall be watered also himself." (Pro. 11:24-25)

"Giving freely and giving with a good heart, will never go unrewarded." (James Clear)

Giving is synonymous with receiving. Giving is sowing and you cannot harvest if you refuse to sow. Giving and receiving is a universal law that nobody can deny. When one witholds his substance from God, he is wilfully blocking God's blessing from coming into his life. Witholding your substances from God will not make you any richer. Some may ask if giving money in the church is necessary, considering that God does not need money. Yes, giving in the church is necessary because the money is channelled into various uses in the church.

Examples are hospitality, helping the poor, widows and the fatherless, supporting needy brethren facing hard times and such like. The church is also maintained and bills are paid from this offerings. The church, as a corporate institution, runs an administrative machinery that must be maintained and properly administered. All this cost money. When we give in church, we must give as unto God; for the work of God.

When you refuse to give to God, you are stagnating your blessings. When you faithfully give unto God, he blesses what you have and bring about more increase. You cannot outgive God. Whatever you give to God will be multiplied back to you many fold. It is our ignorance of the Lordship of Christ over the things we have that makes us think we can withold anything we have from God. If you give bountifully, you shall also reap boutifully.

"Give, and it shall be given unto you; good measure, pressed down, and shaken together, and running over, shall men give into your bosom. For with the same measure that ye mete withal it shall be measured to you again." (Luke 6:38)

Here are promises of blessings that cannot be wished away. All that God wants is blessings for His children. He wants to take us to the flood stage where out of our bellies will flow rivers of living waters. (John 7:38) God is telling you to give to Him so He can multiply it back to you.

In giving, we must do so proportionally, sacrificially and individually.

"Upon the first day of the week let every one of you lay by him in store, as God hath prospered him, that there be no gatherings when I come." (1 Cor. 16:2)

Depending on the day or week one receives his income, one must endevour to put something aside for the work of God. This is the seed that God will multiply back to you. The giving must be proportional; according to the income we make. God does not only look at what we have given. He also look at what is in our pockets and bank accounts. You must have an appreciative spirit as an individual to realize it is God who has given us the power to become wealthy. We must thank him always.

"But thou shalt remember the LORD thy God: for it is He that giveth thee power to get wealth, that He may establish His covenant which He sware unto thy fathers, as it is this day." (Deut. 8:18)

You must give cheerfully without any grumbling because God loveth a cheerful giver.

94

"Every man according as he purpose in his heart, so let him give; not grudgingly, or of necessity: for God loveth a cheerful giver"(2 Cor. 9:7)

Any giving that is done with grudging and complaining does not bring blessing. You should be happy that you are giving to God. When you consider the favor of God upon your life, you will need to really give to God with joy. Don't give as if you are being forced. Give because you love God. Remember God did not hesitate to send Christ to redeem us from sin; that is how much he loves us.

Giving is by itself a form of sacrifice. It is a sacrifice because you are giving away something that you could use yourself. (2 Cor.8:1-4) Treat that sacrifice properly and with respect because you are giving it to God. Whatever you are giving to God as tithes, freewill offerings and other monies or material things must be given sacrificially and be of good quality. If something is not good for your friend or the governor, then certainly such a gift is not good for God.

"And if ye offer the blind for sacrifice, is it not evil? offer it now unto thy governor: will he be pleased with thee, or accept thy person? saith the LORD of hosts."(Mal. 1:8)

Your offerings are a tribute and gratitude to honor God for all that He has done and is still doing for you. Remember your barns shall be full when you give to God.

"Honour the LORD with thy substance, and with the firstfruits of all thine increase:

So shall thy barns be filled with plenty, and thy presses shall burst out with new wine." (Prov. 3: 9-10)

SUMMING UP

"Successful people begin where failures leave off. Never settle for "Just getting the job done." Excel" (Tom Hopkins)

"Build your own dreams or someone else will hire you to build theirs." (Farrah Gray)

"Failure will never overtake me if my determination to succeed is strong enough." (Og Mandino)

When one appraises what has been said so far, the sum total of the truth is that poverty is an evil which must be rooted out. It is not enough to hate poverty. Hating it will not stop it; fighting it will. The crimes of poverty are avoidable crimes. A man doesn't have to steal or beg before he can eat. Individuals need to change their mindset. Society must change it's policies concerning poverty. Enabling enviroment should be created for people to discover and develop their potentials. While crime by poor people or anybody for that matter cannot be justified on any grounds, it is pertinent to note that the minority rich will not sleep in peace so long as the majority poor are awake.

People should put value on their lives. It is the duty of every person to improve his life so he can be useful to himself and society. It will be an act of wilful neglect for an individual to make a cemetary of his life by burying his talents and potentials; potentials that would take the person to a better and purposeful living. If a man is poor, it is just logical that he will do everything to get out of it and not just resign himself to it. One must fight it in the mind, soul and body, and in the enviroment and the society at large.

They say some are born with silver spoons. No problem. If you didn't come with a silver spoon, make one. If you were born in a poor home, you must desire to make that home a better place. You have been born and that is important. What you are now and what you hope to be should be of importance to you. Change every thought of "Failure runs in our family" to "Riches run in our family" Make a catalogue of people who rose from grass to grace and learn from their experience.

People should use the power of creative imaginations to put things on ground and must not give up on projects when they face teething problems. There is an incubation period for every project. If allowed proper time, every dream will translate to reality and fruition. Poverty should not put you down; rather, it should stir your spirit to aspire to acquire. Most people would have made it to the top if they have waited a year longer, a week longer or maybe even a day longer. Unfortunately they gave up just when success was about to smile on them.

One must be organized in his daily life. Most people are not organized in any way. They are behind in everything. If they have a car, they are always searching for the keys when going out. If they have to catch a bus, they are always late. If they have to attend a meeting they are always behind schedule. Their shops always open late for business. Their children are always late for school. Their houses are in disarray. Everything about them is confusion. There is no way one can make any headway when one is not organized.

If you think poverty and failure runs in your family, tell yourself you will do something to change the situation. What you believe most often than not governs your life. Man is the product of his own thoughts; he becomes what he thinks. Refuse to go along with shallow minded people who never believes there is a way out of bad situations. The story of Jabez in 1st Chronicles 4:9-10 offers a valuable lesson.

"And Jabez was more honorable than his brethren: and his mother called his name Jabez, saying, Because I bare him with sorrow.

And Jabez called on the God of Israel, saying, Oh that thou wouldest bless me indeed, and enlarge my coast, and that thine hand might be with me, and that thou wouldest keep me from evil, that it may not grieve me! And God granted him that which he requested."

Here was a man born in adversity. The situation was so bad his mother named him Jabez– "child of sorrow" While his brothers resigned themselves to the adverse situation in the family, Jabez made a choice– "I chose to change." His prayer was simply that God would bless him, enlarge his coasts and keep him from evil so he will not be grieved. God granted him his request and he was counted more honorable than his brethren.

Look at yourself and the enviroment and see the devastating effects of poverty. This should motivate you to do something about it. Like Jabez, you can make the difference in your family. Set up goals in your life and work towards achieving them. If the name you bear is contributing to a negative mindset in your life, the sensible thing to do is change that name. If Jabez has folded his hands and did nothing like his brothers, he would have been yet another poor canditate just added to the long list of a family of non achievers. Jabez is a winner any day. His example should ignite a passion for success in every person who desires a positive change.

SOME FOOD FOR THOUGHT

"I know the price of success. Dedication, hard work and an unremitting devotion to the things you want to see happen." (Frank Lloyd Wright)

"Successful people have fears. Successful people have doubts. Successful people have worries. They just don't let these feelings stop them." (T. Harv Eker)

"Success seems to be connected with action. Successful people keep moving. They make mistakes, but they don't quit." (Conrad Hilton)

According to the United Nations World Food Programe, hunger is the body's way of signalling that it is running short of food and needs to eat something. Hunger can lead to malnutrition.

UNDER-NOURISHMENT describes the status of people whose food intake does not include enough calories (energy) to meet minimum phisiological needs.

MALNUTRITION / UNDER-NUTRITION is defined as a state in which the physical function of an individual is impaired to the point where he or she can no longer maintain natural body capabilities; such as growth, pregnancy, lactation, learning abilities, physical work, resisting and recovering from disease. The term covers a range of problems from being dangerously thin (under- weight) or too short (stunting) for one's age to being deficient in vitamins and minerals or being too fat. (obese)

STUNTING reflects shortness- for age. It is an indicator of chronic malnutrition and is calculated by comparing the height with the age of a child with a reference population of well nourished and healthy children.

WASTING reflects a recent and severe process that has led to substantial weight loss, usually associated with starvation and or disease. It is calculated by comparing weight-for-height of a child with a reference population of well nourished and healthy children. It is often used to access the severity of emergencies because it is strongly related to mortality

UNDER-WEIGHT is measured by comparing the weight for age of a child with a refernce population of well nourished and healthy children.

The United States Department of Agriculture describes FOOD SECURITY as assured access to enough nutrition to sustain an active and healthy life with dignity.

FOOD INSECURITY is a condition of uncertain availability of or ability to acquire safe nutritions and food in a socially acceptable way.

HIGH FOOD SECURITY means there are no reported indication of food access problems or limitations.

MARGINAL FOOD SECURITY indicates one or two reported indications of food access problems or limitations- typically of anxiety over food sufficiency or shortage of food in the house. There is little or no indication of changes in diets or food intake.

LOW FOOD SECURITY means there are reports of reduced quality, variety or desirebility or diet. There is little or no indication of reduced food intake.

VERY LOW FOOD SECURITY indicates reports of multiple indication of disrupted eating patterns and reduced food intake.

www.ingramcontent.com/pod-product-compliance
Lightning Source LLC
Chambersburg PA
CBHW030259030426
42336CB00009B/443